A GA

BULBS

Enjoy year-round colour with this selection
of bulbs, corms, tubers and rhizomes

Nerine bowdenii

Colchicum speciosum

A GARDENER'S GUIDE TO

BULBS

Enjoy year-round colour with this selection
of bulbs, corms, tubers and rhizomes

DAVID PAPWORTH

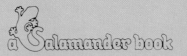

Published by Salamander Books Limited
LONDON

A Salamander Book

Published by Salamander Books Ltd.,
52 Bedford Row,
London WC1R 4LR.

© 1988 Salamander Books Ltd.

ISBN 0 86101 370 0

Distributed by
Hodder and Stoughton Services,
PO Box 6, Mill Road, Dunton Green,
Sevenoaks, Kent TN13 2XX.

All correspondence concerning the
content of this volume should be
addressed to Salamander Books Ltd.

Contents

Text and colour photographs are cross-
referenced throughout as follows: 64 ♦.
The plants are arranged in alphabetical
order of Latin name. Page numbers in
bold refer to text entries; those in *italics*
refer to photographs.

Credits

Author: David Papworth is a freelance writer and illustrator on horticultural subjects. He is also involved in preparing garden designs for show houses, exhibitions and private homes. For a period of over 12 years David was Gardening Editor of Ideal Home magazine. He has written two other books: 'Patios and Water Gardens' (1973) and 'Patios and Windowbox Gardening' (1983). He regularly contributes text and illustrations to gardening and handyman magazines and is a keen and accomplished gardener.

Editor: Geoff Rogers
Designer: Roger Hyde
Colour reproductions: Rodney Howe Ltd., England
Monochrome: Bantam Litho Ltd., England.
Filmset: SX Composing Ltd., England.

Printed in Belgium by Henri Proost & Cie, Turnhout.

Introduction

What exactly are bulbs, corms, rhizomes and tubers; what have they in common; and why are they different?

All these root forms are food storage systems built up in one season when the weather allows nutrients to be readily available, and then used during the following season when the plants need to grow rapidly and flower at a time when drought, frozen soil or other poor growing conditions occur.

A *bulb* is a collection of old leaf bases around an embryo bud and new leaves that will emerge the next season. A *corm* is the thickened end of a stem that will shoot up and produce leaves along its length. A *rhizome* is a horizontal stem – sometimes above ground and at other times below the surface – which will sprout tufts of leaves; sometimes it runs under the ground and emerges some distance from the parent plant. A *tuber* is a swollen root that stores goodness for the coming year.

Most of these plants produce underground offshoots that can be removed and grown on separately to become mature plants. Bulbs often produce small bulbs around the root area, called *bulblets,* which can be separated and replanted in protected nursery beds. Corms produce a new corm either above or next to the old one, and often smaller ones are also produced, which can be treated like bulblets to reach maturity. Rhizomes and tubers are usually divided by cutting but each piece must have an eye or small shoot to grow; if there is a root system as well, each section must have some rooting growth in order to survive.

Buying bulbs

There are many places for buying bulbs – garden centres, nurseries, supermarkets and mail order specialists – and it is quite a simple matter to find what you are looking for; but do be wary of cheap offers, for in this field you get only what you pay for, and other people's rejects are often disposed of in this way. It is better to buy one good bulb than a dozen poor ones.

Left: **Tulip 'Bing Crosby'**
A Triumph tulip grown from a bulb that produces a plain red bloom, but colour breaking can occur. 152◗

Below: *Four types of food reservoir: (A) Bulb (leaf storage); (B) Corm (stem supply); (C) Rhizome (swollen stem) and (D) Tuber (enlarged root).*

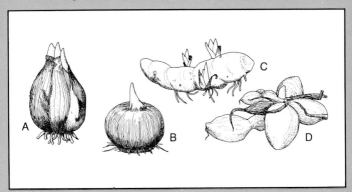

Bulbs come in different sizes and forms. In the narcissus family there are 'mother' bulbs, which will produce a number of shoots and flowers, and can then be divided up to give several individual bulbs. 'Double nose' bulbs should give two shoots and flowers. Offsets are unlikely to be mature enough to flower in the first year. Some suppliers give quantity discounts, and these should be treated as genuine bargains and not confused with cheap offers. Bruised or damaged bulbs, or ones that show signs of insect attack or mould, should be avoided where possible. Spare bulbs from friends or neighbours may carry disease and pests; if you use them, give the bulbs and the surrounding soil a dose of pesticide and fungicide.

Storing bulbs
At the end of the growing season it is sometimes necessary to lift and store bulbs. They should be sorted, named and treated with a fungicide. Some will need to be covered with moist peat, but others will require a dry covering. Keep them in a cool place that is frost-free, not too dry (or the bulbs will shrivel) and protected against marauding pests such as mice. Inspect your store of bulbs during the winter and remove any that are beginning to rot or show disease. Tubers that are drying out and look shrivelled can be soaked in water overnight, then dried on the surface and replaced in store. By taking care during the winter months you should have healthy bulbs to plant when the season is right.

Health
To keep disease and pest attack to a minimum it is best to prevent trouble before it starts, by treating the plant and the surrounding soil with an appropriate preparation. This can be a chemical, but for

Above: **Crocus 'Firefly'**
Crocuses grow from a corm, the thickened end of the stem that will release food when nutrition is short.

Above: **Iris innominata**
An American beardless iris grown from a rhizome, a swollen underground stem. 87♦

those who have deep feelings against chemicals there are natural products that will help to fend off any attack. Whether they are man-made or natural, treat every such product with respect, and keep to the manufacturer's instructions. A solution may look weak, but resist the temptation to make it stronger; it is when we fail to use the right dose that trouble starts. As a general rule, a good healthy plant will keep disease at bay and shrug off a few pests; it is the weak plants that attract trouble and then spread it around.

Planting
Before planting takes place, a little preparation is important. First, plan where the bulbs are to be placed, how many, and in what shape or order. Once this is decided, then the area of soil can be prepared and dug over, all weed roots removed and drainage supplied if necessary: often a good dose of bulky manure, sharp sand or leaf-mould is sufficient to open the texture of the soil and improve the drainage. Peat can be added where there is a need for more moisture; this, together with manure and leaf-mould, can be either dug well in or left as a thick layer or mulch on the surface, but do take care that manure is not in direct contact with the bulb and that the manure used is old and well rotted. Where the soil is boggy a series of land drains should be laid to drain the soil; if this is impossible, it is better to use the land to good advantage, and make a bog garden planted with moisture-loving specimens.

Feeding

It is important to provide food each season, so that every plant will have built up strength to produce leaves and flowers during the next growth period. In most cases, feeding takes place either when the leaves are mature and can absorb nourishment even if the flowers have finished blooming, or – in the case of the colchicum – before the flowers appear. A surface dressing of a general fertilizer will be washed into the soil by the rain and taken up by the roots. A mulch of compost will follow the same path with the added advantage of supplying humus to improve the soil. A good dose of liquid manure will feed the plant through its leaves as well as through its roots. All these types of feed will do wonders to the plant, fattening up the roots and storage growths for the next year, when the size and blooms will be much improved. Watering is important, too; make sure that the bulb is kept moist during the feeding period. If drought occurs, check that the soil has not dried out, and if it has, give a copious draught so that the soil is thoroughly soaked down to the bulb roots. A mere sprinkle of water will just dampen the surface and encourage the roots to grow towards the moisture, which will quickly dry out.

Propagation

In general the increase of plants occurs naturally through seed, by increase of roots, or by *layering* (stems touch the soil and develop a new root system, and gradually become independent). In most cases bulbs produce small bulblets around the parent bulb, which grow into full-sized ones in a year or two; these should replace other bulbs that are lost through age, disease, drought, pests or poor conditions. Plants grown from seed will in some cases take six years or more to reach the flowering stage, and for most of us this is far too long to wait – even waiting for bulblets to produce blooms is some-times more than we can bear, so we have to resort to buying bulbs to give us instant gardens. Even if we purchase bulbs, however, we can still keep a small bed of bulblets or even a pot in a sheltered part of the garden. To keep the young plants from being choked with weeds, grow them in a sterilized potting mixture. This will give them a balanced soil to grow in, a good start in life, and a better chance to reach maturity. Where seed is recommended for increasing stock, a seed-growing mixture should be used and the instructions given in the text of this book should be followed.

Indoor forcing

To provide blooms out of season or even a few weeks earlier the bulb growers have devised a system of cultivation using cold and warm storage, so that spring flowers are available during the winter months. Plant them in containers of peat and charcoal, provide them with moisture, and keep them in the dark to sprout. When the shoot has emerged from the bulb and grown to the desired length bring the plants out into the light and warmth, where they will bloom. After flowering they can be planted out in the garden, but some bulbs take a long time to recover their natural cycle. Many bulbs suitable for growing indoors are sold complete with pot and soil.

Selection

The plants featured in this book have been selected to give a broad range of different types, and most are readily available commercially. They include hardy, half-hardy and tender forms. Hardy plants will survive in the colder regions of the temperate zone, and can withstand prolonged frost and moderately hot weather. Half-hardy ones are from warmer regions of the temperate area, stand up to the occasional frost, and thrive in heat. Tender types are best kept to areas where there is little frost or where protection can be given. In the case of dormant bulbs a thick layer of straw, compost, bracken or peat will insulate them. In colder areas it is best to treat the tender plants as pot specimens to be kept in the greenhouse or indoors. The choice of plants in this book gives a variety of flower, leaf and size; you should be able to find plants that you can fit into existing schemes without having to alter the planting to see the new varieties. There are small subjects suitable for the alpine garden as well as for the border, larger ones for the back of the herbaceous border, and middle-sized ones that can stand on their own or be mixed with other plants. Whichever sort you choose you can have flowers the whole year round provided you pick the right varieties.

Names given are, in most cases, the Latin ones that are known in all countries; the common names vary from district to district. The most common names are given after the Latin name to help identification. The planting depths indicate the distance between the top of the bulb and the soil surface.

Below: **Dahlia 'Scaur Princess'**
A decorative dahlia that is a fine example of a tuberous plant; the swollen root system feeds the plant when it cannot draw nutrition from the soil. Protect from frost. 53-57▶

Above:
Agapanthus campanulatus
This plant forms a delightful focal point in the garden, with its sword-like leaves and delicate blooms. Ideal for border or containers. 18♦

Above: **Alstroemeria aurantiaca**
The rich colour and exotic markings of this plant contrast with the blue-grey leaves in summer. Place it in a sheltered site in full sun. 20♦

Below: **Amaryllis belladonna**
An exotic plant that is ideal in a sheltered border or among shrubs, where the large blooms make a fine spectacle in late summer. 21♦

Above:
Anemone blanda 'Blue Pearl'
This fine low-growing plant brightens up the border and rock garden in late winter and early spring with its finely shaped blooms. It forms a clump and will grow happily in either sun or shade and in a well-drained soil. 21♦

Left: **Anemone coronaria**
The cultivated anemone that every florist stocks; available in a variety of colours with dark centres. They are very popular as garden plants and will grow well in the border as well as in the rock garden. 22♦

Right: **Anemone nemorosa**
This plant enjoys the light shade provided by thin woodland and forms a low-growing mass. Where the soil is moist it will increase and produce a prolific display of white flowers in early spring. 22♦

Above: **Begonia × tuberhybrida**
*A fine example of the picotee
begonia, which is noted for its
delicate edging along the petals in a
contrasting colour. They are ideal for
bedding plants, and in containers
and hanging baskets, where they
provide a touch of vivid colour. Avoid
too much sun.* 24-5♦

Left: **Begonia × tuberhybrida**
*The rich colour of the large blooms
stands out against the dark green
leaves and, provided it is kept out of
too much sun and is given a moist
soil and high humidity it will reward
the owner with a succession of
blooms from early summer to late
autumn. A pot or bedding plant.* 24-5♦

Achimenes heterophylla

- **Light position, but avoid strong sunshine**
- **Soil on the dry side**
- **Plant tubers 2.5cm (1in) deep**

This tender tuberous bushy plant has mid-green, toothed and hairy leaves, borne in threes, that drop in the autumn. In a greenhouse, it will grow to 30cm (12in). The long-lasting flowers start trumpet shaped, opening out to flat pansy-like blooms in shades of bright orange and crimson, almost 4cm (1.6in) across.

Using a peat-based mixture place the tubers 2.5cm (1in) deep in a flowerpot, six to a 12.5cm (5in) pot, and gently moisten the mixture. Once tubers have sprouted, feed them with liquid fertilizer every two weeks, keeping the plant at 16°C 60°F). Support the plant with canes or string. Keep the foliage out of strong sun, misting the leaves with water in hot weather. In autumn allow the plant to dry out, and then place in a frost-free position until spring. These plants are generally pest- and disease-free.

Take care
Avoid direct fierce sunlight and overwatering.

Acidanthera bicolor murielae

(Sweet-scented gladiolus)
- **Sunny sheltered position**
- **Any garden soil that is not waterlogged**
- **Plant 10cm (4in) deep**

This half-hardy plant will not stand frost reaching the corm. It should be either grown as a greenhouse subject or used for bedding unless in a very sheltered frost-free area. It will grow to 90cm (36in), with sword-shaped leaves. In late summer the scented star-shaped flowers appear, up to eight per stem, white with deep purple centres, about 5cm (2in) across.

Plant the corms in any garden soil with reasonable drainage, at a depth of 10cm (4in) in spring, about 20cm (8in) apart, in a sunny position. Lift the plants before the first hard frost and dry them off in the greenhouse. Separate young corms from the parent corm and keep them all in a warm dry place until spring. For greenhouse use put up to six in a 15cm (6in) pot in winter for midsummer blooms. Use pesticides to stop slugs and thrips.

Take care
Keep corms frost-free, and grow in a well-drained soil.

Agapanthus campanulatus
- Sunny position
- Well-drained soil
- Plant crowns 5cm (2in) deep

This fleshy-rooted plant grows in clumps of sword-like foliage that die back in winter to emerge again the following spring. Plants grow up to 75cm (30in) tall and should be 45cm (18in) apart. The late summer flowers are in ball-like groups on the end of tall stems almost 1m (39in) long, and vary in colour from white to amethyst.

They thrive in a warm sunny position with well-drained soil, but most withstand winter frosts. When the flowers die back, cut the stems to ground level, and cover the crowns with bracken, compost, straw or ashes if sited in a frost pocket. The roots can be lifted, divided and replanted in late spring; growing fresh stock from seed takes up to three years from sowing to flowering. Seeds should be sown in spring in seed mixture at 13-16°C (55-60°F); transplant them to boxes and on to flowerpots as they mature. Overwinter in a frost-free place and plant out in late spring.

Take care
Do not plant in waterlogged soil. 12◆

Allium giganteum
- Sunny site
- Well-drained soil
- Plant with 15cm (6in) of soil above bulb

This bulbous plant is grown mainly for its decorative flowerhead, which stands well above other herbaceous plants. The leaves are grey-blue and strap-like, making a clump up to 45cm (18in) in height, with flowerheads 10cm (4in) across. The flowers in midsummer are deep lilac. As soon as the flowers die, cut the heads off but leave the stalks to feed the bulb for the following year; dead leaves and stems should be removed in autumn.

Grow them in a sunny place in well-drained soil, and leave untouched for a few years; then lift, split and replant in spring or autumn with more space around the bulbs. Seeds can be sown in autumn, winter or spring; leave them for 12 months, then replant in nursery rows out of doors, keeping the soil moist.

Watch for slugs and white rot. Infected bulbs should be destroyed, and the soil dusted with calomel dust. Do not grow alliums there for 10 years.

Take care
Stake plants on windy sites.

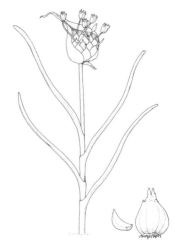

Allium moly
- **Sunny site**
- **Well-drained soil**
- **Plant with 7.5cm (3in) of soil over the bulb**

This allium is suitable for the rock garden, as it grows only 30cm (12in) tall. It has strap-like grey leaves, and bright yellow star-like flowers that form clusters 5cm (2in) wide on the end of the flower stems in midsummer. The plants spread 15cm (6in) across and should be planted this distance apart.

Plant the bulbs in autumn in well-drained soil with some moisture; they prefer a sunny site. Leave them for a few years, until the flowers become crowded; then lift the clump in spring or autumn, split and replant with more space. This can be grown as a pot plant provided it is kept cool until the flower buds start to open and then it can be brought indoors. Sow seeds in winter or spring, and after 12 months replant in a nursery bed for another two years.

Protect from slugs, and watch for white rot. If white fungus appears at the base of the bulbs, destroy the plants and do not grow alliums in this soil for 10 years.

Take care
Avoid waterlogged soil.

Allium sativum
(Garlic)
- **Sunny position**
- **Moist light soil fed with manure**
- **Plant 15cm (6in) deep; cloves 7.5cm (3in) deep**

Garlic is a member of the onion family and grows to 60cm (24in) tall, with narrow grey-green leaves. The bulb itself is made up of several segments known as cloves, which are held together with a thin dryish skin. The plant has heads of tiny white blooms flushed with red at midsummer; remove these to keep the bulbs well-formed.

Garlic thrives in a light soil that has manure in it to keep the bulbs moist and fed. They are ready for harvesting in late summer. Plant bulbs in winter at a depth of 15cm (6in), but if cloves are used instead of bulbs, keep 7.5cm (3in) of soil over them. When the leaves turn yellow in summer, the bulbs can be lifted and laid out in the sun to dry; then they can be stored for the winter in a cool but frost-free place. Pick out the best bulbs for planting next season. Garlic is generally pest-free, but if it is attacked by fungus disease, destroy the plant to stop it spreading.

Take care
Keep the soil moist during the growing season.

Allium schoenoprasum
(Chives)
- **Full sun or partial shade**
- **Good soil**
- **Plant 1.25cm (0.5in) deep**

This hardy perennial herb, used in the kitchen for flavouring, produces a clump of hollow grass-like leaves. In midsummer the spherical flowers appear, rose-pink in colour and 2.5-4cm (1-1.6in) across.

Chives should be grown in a good soil in full sun or partial shade. In dry periods, water the plant to keep it moist. To keep a supply of leaves, all flowers should be removed. The plants die back in winter and resprout the following spring. Use cloches to cover the plants in winter, to get early leaves to pick in spring. Spread compost or manure over the area in spring. Plants can be divided in autumn and replanted to give more space. At this time, lift one or two clumps and put them into pots; kept on the kitchen windowsill they will provide fresh leaves through the winter. Chives are normally pest- and disease-free.

Take care
Pinch out flowerheads to give a continuous supply of leaves.

Alstroemeria aurantiaca
- **Sunny, sheltered site**
- **Well-drained fertile soil**
- **Plant tubers 10-15cm (4-6in) deep**

This tuberous-rooted plant has twisted blue-grey leaves, and grows to a height of 90cm (36in). Borne on leafy stems, the flowers are trumpet-shaped in orange-reds, the upper two petals having red veins.

Plant the tubers in spring. Cover with a mulch of compost or well-rotted manure in spring. As they grow, support to prevent them being blown over. Dead-head plants to encourage more blooms. In autumn cut stems down to the ground. In spring the plants can be divided, but take care not to disturb the roots unduly. Sometimes the plant will not produce any stems, leaves or flowers during the first season, but once established it can be left for years. Sow seed in spring in a cold frame, and plant out a year later.

Watch for slugs and caterpillars, and use a suitable insecticide if necessary. When the plant shows yellow mottling and distorted growth, destroy it – this is a virus disease.

Take care
Avoid damaging the roots. 13♦

Amaryllis belladonna
- **Sunny sheltered position**
- **Well-drained soil**
- **Plant 15-20cm (6-8in) deep**

This bulbous plant has strap-like leaves, lasting from late winter through to midsummer. After the leaves die down, flower stems appear and grow to a height of 75cm (30in). The trumpet-shaped fragrant pink or white flowers vary from three to 12 on a stem.

Plant the bulbs in summer in a warm sheltered situation in well-drained soil. Bulbs can be divided in summer and should be replanted immediately. Dead-head the flowers as they fade, and remove leaves and stems as they die.

Hippeastrum bulbs, often sold as Amaryllis, are tender indoor subjects. Plant one bulb in a 15-20cm (6-8in) pot of well-draining mixture, leaving a third of the bulb exposed. Water a little until the flower stem appears and then water and feed liberally. Bulbs bloom about three months after planting. Prepared bulbs planted in late autumn flower during midwinter.

Take care
Keep moist when transplanting. 13♦

Anemone blanda
(Blue windflower)
- **Sun or light shade**
- **Well-drained soil**
- **Plant 5cm (2in) deep**

This spring-flowering plant grows to 15cm (6in) tall; the daisy-like flowers, in white, pink, red-tipped, lavender or pale blue, and 3.5cm (1.4in) across, appear during spring. They make an ideal rockery plant and can be grown in clumps under trees.

They tolerate either alkaline or acid soils provided they are well-drained. Corms should be planted 10cm (4in) apart in autumn. Lift the corms after leaves die down in early autumn; divide, and remove offsets for replanting. Sow seeds in late summer, and germinate in a cold frame; transplant seedlings, and grow on for two years before moving to final positions.

If plant and soil are treated with a general insecticide you should have little trouble. Stunted yellow leaves and meagre flowers indicate a virus attack; destroy plants before the virus can spread.

Take care
Soak corms for 48 hours before planting. 14-15♦

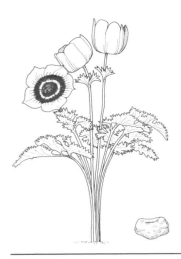 

Anemone coronaria

- **Sunny or lightly shaded position**
- **Well-drained soil**
- **Plant corms 5cm (2in) deep**

This E Mediterranean plant flowers in spring, and the blooms vary from white to blue or red. From this plant have developed the De Caen and the new robust St. Piran, both with single flowers, and the St. Brigid anemone with double or semi-double blooms. These grow to a height of 30cm (12in) and flowers are up to 7.5cm (3in) across.

Corms should be planted in early autumn, 15cm (6in) apart; by planting in other months a succession of blooms can be had throughout the year. Corms deteriorate, and should be replaced every couple of years. Anemones can be grown from seed, sown in late summer and kept in a cold frame. Transplant the seedlings, leave for a year, and then move to their flowering position. Treat these plants with a general pesticide to stop insect attack. If the plant looks sick and the leaves turn yellow, destroy it before the virus spreads.

Take care
Replace corms every other year. 14♦

Anemone nemorosa

(Wood anemone)
- **Light shade**
- **Well-drained soil with leaf-mould**
- **Plant 5cm (2in) deep**

This anemone has white flowers with a touch of pink or blue on the outside of the petals. The low-growing plant reaches 10cm (4in) high, although some varieties grow to twice this size. The flowers are single, about 2.5cm (1in) across, but there are some double varieties.

These plants are easily grown from corms, provided they are planted in autumn in a shady place with moist soil, and they will bloom in spring. They may be attacked by a number of insects, such as flea beetles, caterpillars, cut worms, aphids or slugs. These should be treated with a suitable insecticide when damage is seen. Virus and rust disease can affect the plants, leaving yellow spores on the leaves and stems and yellowing of leaves with twisted flowers; if either of these symptoms is seen, destroy the plant.

Take care
Do not plant in a hot dry position. 15♦

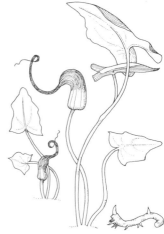

Arisaema speciosum
- Shady woodland
- Moist soil with leaf-mould
- Plant 15cm (6in) deep

Arisarum prosciodeum
(Mouse plant)
- Shady area
- Moist fibrous soil
- Plant 15cm (6in) deep

Originating from the E Himalayan forests, this tuberous plant has mid-green leaves edged with red, and unusual flowers. The true flowers are very small, and form around the base of a central pencil-like stem that tapers to a length of 50cm (20in); this is surrounded by a petal-like spathe 15cm (6in) long and 10cm (4in) wide, striped in purple and white. The plant grows to a height of 45cm (18in) excluding the flower stem. The flowers appear in late spring.

The tubers should be planted in summer in a moist, shady place where there is plenty of leaf-mould in the soil. Cover the area with a layer of bracken to protect the plants during winter. When necessary, lift the plant in late summer, divide and replant with more space. Generally arisaemas are pest-free, but treat with a fungicide to prevent the roots from rotting.

Take care
Watch for root rot in heavy wet soils.

This plant thrives in woodland areas where it is partially shaded. It will grow to 12.5cm (5in) tall, but it spreads to form a dense mat of arrow-shaped leaves under which the mouse-like flowers are borne in late spring, lasting until late summer. The flowers are the size and shape of a mouse, joined to the stem at the 'head' end, and the colour is a mouse brown.

These plants are hardy and easy to grow in a moist soil containing plenty of humus; too much sun would dry up the plant. Tubers should be planted in autumn, 15cm (6in) deep. When they are established, they can be lifted and divided, and the offsets removed, in spring. They should be replanted before the root system dries out; this will enable the plant to settle before new growth appears. The arisarum is generally both pest- and disease-free.

Take care
Plant where there is both moisture and shade.

Arum italicum
- Partial shade
- Well-drained soil with leaf-mould
- Plant 7.5cm (3in) deep

This hardy perennial grows to a height of 30cm (12in) from a rhizome. Large heavily marbled leaves in white and dark green appear in autumn. In spring there are unusual creamy-green flowers, followed in autumn by bright red berries that are 1.25cm (0.5in) across, grouped on compact spikes 15cm (6in) long.

Plant in summer in a dry soil that has plenty of humus added in the form of leaf-mould; the rhizome should be planted 7.5cm (3in) deep in semi-shade. In severe winters a mulch of compost, leaf-mould or bracken spread over the plants will protect them against hard frost. To increase stock the seeds can be sown when they are ripe in autumn; or the plant can be lifted in the summer, divided and offsets removed, and replanted. Normally the plant is free from pests but the root is susceptible to rot from excess moisture; treat soil with fungicide.

Take care
Keep the soil well-drained.

Begonia ×
tuberhybrida
- Slight shade
- Humid atmosphere, moist soil
- Plant flush with the soil

The parents of this tuberous-rooted group come from China, Japan and Socotra, an island in the Indian Ocean. The plants form a very popular series of hybrids or crosses with large rose-like flowers and mid-green ear-shaped leaves. The plants grow to 60cm (24in) tall, with a spread of 45cm (18in). Both male and female flowers are borne on the same plant: the females are single blooms, but the males are more noticeable, being double in form and 7.5-15cm (3-6in) across. They flower from summer to late autumn, and are very popular as both bedding and pot plants. The range of colours is wide, with brilliant hues of yellow, orange, reds, pink and white; some have bands of red edging to the petals, and are known as picotee begonias.

The tubers are started in damp peat when a temperature of 16°C (60°F) can be kept, the tubers being placed just level with the surface and with the flat or slightly hollow surface uppermost. As the leaves start shooting, the tuber should be lifted

Begonia × tuberhybrida
The drawing shows one of the very attractive picotee begonias, with blooms edged in a darker colour.

Begonia × tuberhybrida
The pendulous hybrid shown in the drawing has relatively small flowers borne profusely on slender stems.

and put into a pot with moist growing medium. As the roots fill the pot, move to a larger container and support the stems with a cane. Once established the pots should be given an occasional liquid feed. At the end of spring the danger of frost should have passed and they can be planted out in the open.

To retain deep colours, keep the plant out of direct sunshine and prevent over-heating by spraying it with water. Larger flowers can be produced by removing the single female blooms and allowing only one shoot to each tuber; remove the other shoots and use them as cuttings. Push these into a sharp soil and keep moist until rooted. Sow seeds in winter at the same temperature as when tubers are started and you should get flowers the same year; tubers will be formed and they can be kept for the following year. At the end of the growing season, when the leaves start to turn yellow or the first frost occurs, the plants can be lifted and kept in a frost-free place until they have died

back. The tubers can be separated from the dead leaves and stem, and stored in peat where there is protection from frost through the winter until the following year, when they can be started off again on their next cycle.

Pendent varieties are ideal for hanging baskets, containers and windowboxes where they can spill over the edge. The winter-flowering Lorraine begonias are grown in spring from cuttings and should be kept at 10°C (50°F) for the flowers to continue throughout the winter. These plants should be kept just moist. When growing from seed, mix the seeds with some fine sand, spread the mixture over the surface of the seed-growing medium, press down and put no additional soil on top; this will even the distribution of the seeds. Begonias can also be propagated by dividing the tubers, or by leaf cuttings. Keep pests to a minimum with a general pesticide; diseases are generally due to over-wet conditions encouraging moulds, so use a fungicide too. 16, 33◆

Begonia boweri
(Eyelash begonia)
- **Moist and shady**
- **Frost-free place in winter**
- **Plant on the surface**

This very small evergreen begonia grows from a rhizome. It is cultivated for its small decorative hairy leaves, which are emerald-green with a margin of dark brown blotches. The white or pale rose flowers are only 1.25cm (0.5in) across and appear in spring in small groups. They can be increased by dividing the rhizome in spring, making sure each section has a healthy growing point. Treat as pot plants, or use for windowboxes and outside containers.

Seeds should be sown in early spring at 16°C (60°F). As the seeds are very fine, mix them with some sand before sowing; do not cover the seeds with soil. Once plants are large enough to handle, transplant into pots or boxes. They can be put out into the open in late spring for flowering.

Avoid pests by treating soil and plant with a general pesticide. Disease attack is usually mould or fungus, encouraged by the warm moist conditions, so use a fungicide.

Take care
Make sure plants are shaded.

Begonia masoniana
(Iron Cross begonia)
- **Light shade**
- **Light soil with peat**
- **Plant flush with the surface**

This attractive evergreen begonia is grown for its foliage. The ear-shaped leaves are tightly crinkled, hairy and bright green, with a cross pattern of dark purplish bars. It grows to a height of 23cm (9in) and a spread of 30cm (12in), and it rarely flowers.

It grows from a rhizome and can be increased in spring by dividing the rhizome into pieces, making sure that each has a growing point. This begonia is usually grown as a pot plant, but do not place it in a room with a gas fire, as the fumes can kill it. It prefers a warm moist soil, and some shade from direct sunlight. When it becomes pot-bound, move it to a larger pot at any time from spring to autumn. During winter the plant should be kept just moist – not too much, or rot will occur.

A general pesticide will keep insects away, and a fungicide will deter the fungus and mould infections attracted to the warm moist conditions.

Take care
Keep moist in summer, but almost dry in winter.

Begonia rex
- **Light shade**
- **Light moist soil**
- **Plant just flush with the surface**

These begonias can be used as pot specimens or as bedding plants. They grow to 30cm (12in) high, and spread to 45cm (18in). The leaf colour can vary, with silver markings on dark green to a spectrum of yellows, reds, creams and purples in bands and patterns. Occasionally pale rose flowers, 1.25cm (0.5in) across, appear during summer.

This begonia prefers a light shade: direct sun can bleach the colour, and dry out the plant in summer. In winter it needs a frost-free situation with a little water to keep the plant moist — too much, and the plant can be affected by rot and mildew. Propagate by leaf cuttings, or even sections of leaves about 5cm (2in) square can be placed on moist peat at a temperature of 21°C (70°F) and will develop roots from the underside. *B. rex* can also be grown from seeds, sown in early spring at 16°C (60°F) and transplanted when the first true leaf appears.

Take care
Syringe the plants with water if summer heat makes them wilt.

Brodiaea laxa
- **Sunny position**
- **Well-drained soil**
- **Plant 7.5cm (3in) deep**

These plants have long narrow leaves, and trumpet flowers on leafless stems. They grow up to 60cm (24in) tall, with flowers of blue, mauve or white, almost 4cm (1.6in) across, from spring to midsummer.

Brodiaeas prefer a heavy soil in a warm place, and show well when treated as a drift, the corms 15cm (6in) apart, or planted in clumps. Plant corms in late summer in well-drained soil or in pots. Soak well with water after planting, and keep just moist until the first leaf appears; they should be kept well watered until flowering has finished, then let them dry. The plants should be lifted every few years; divide the corms and replant with more space around them. They can be grown from seed but take up to five years to mature. They are generally both pest- and disease-free.

Take care
Do not overwater after flowering.

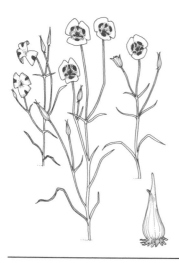

Calochortus venustus

(Mariposa lily)
- **Full sun**
- **Dry, well-drained sandy soil**
- **Plant 7.5cm (3in) deep**

These bulbous plants thrive in light woodland and open grassland; in light sandy soil they grow to over 45cm (18in) tall. The calochortus forms a spindly plant with insignificant foliage of long slender leaves that appear in early spring; the summer flowers vary from white to yellow, orange, rose, dark red or purple, with very decorative markings, and reach 5cm (2in) across.

Plant in autumn in a sunny situation, with a dry sandy soil that has some leaf-mould in it. The bulbs should be planted 7.5cm (3in) deep and kept away from excessive moisture, so ensure that the soil is well drained. When foliage dies down keep the plant dry until growth starts again; then keep it just moist until it flowers. It will grow well in a pot in the greenhouse. To keep the plant free from attack, treat with both a pesticide and a fungicide.

Take care
Keep this plant on the dry side. 34♦

Camassia leichtlinii

(Quamash)
- **Sun or light shade**
- **Moist soil**
- **Plant 15cm (6in) deep**

This plant grows to a height of 90cm (36in) and has pointed sword-like leaves. The flowers, on stems that grow above the leaves, are star-shaped in blue or white, about 4cm (1.6in) across, and appear in summer.

This species should be planted in a heavy moist soil with plenty of leaf-mould or peat to prevent drying out by spring winds and summer droughts. The bulbs should be planted in autumn, 15cm (6in) apart. They can be left for a few years; then in autumn lift the bulbs, split up and replant to give them more space. To prevent strength being taken from the bulbs, dead flowerheads should be removed. To increase your stock, bulblets can be removed from around the older bulbs in early autumn and replanted immediately; they should reach flowering size in three years. Seeds can be sown, but may take up to five years to flower.

Take care
Do not let the bulbs dry out in spring and early summer.

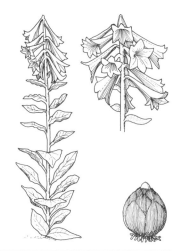

Canna × hybrida
- Sunny and sheltered position
- Rich peaty soil
- Just cover the rhizome

These tropical plants have broad
leaves and bright flowers. The plants
grow to a height of 120cm (4ft) and
should be kept at least 30cm (12in)
apart. Cannas fall into two groups,
those with green leaves and those
with brown to purple ones; the
leaves can be up to 60cm (24in) long
and 30cm (12in) wide. The flowers
are about 7.5cm (3in) long, in brilliant
orange or yellow.

Plant the rhizomes in pots in early
spring, and keep them at 16°C
(60°F). If more than one shoot
appears the rhizome can be divided;
make sure that each section has a
shoot, a piece of rhizome and some
roots. In late spring they can be
planted outside in a sheltered sunny
place. Bring plants indoors before
autumn frosts, and keep in a cool but
not cold place during the winter.
Treat soil and plants with a general
pesticide to deter slugs, leather-
jackets and cutworms. Cannas are
usually disease-free.

Take care
Keep frost-free in winter. 34-5▶

Cardiocrinum giganteum
(Giant lily)
- Sheltered, in light shade
- Well-drained but rich soil
- Plant just below the surface

This hardy bulbous perennial has
dark green heart-shaped leaves that
grow in a spiral from ground level to
just below the first flower. The plants
can reach 3m (10ft) high, and should
be planted 90cm (3ft) apart. The
flowers are borne on a long stem in
summer; they consist of a series of
trumpets, often over 15cm (6in)
long, in cream or palest green
streaked with red-brown or purple.

The bulbs die after flowering but
usually leave offset bulbs, which
mature and flower in three to five
years. Sets of bulbs can be bought to
give continuous flowering, and as
the last bulb dies the first's offsets
are ready to flower. Adult bulbs
should be planted in autumn, with
the neck just below the surface.
Water freely in dry spells; a layer of
garden compost or manure spread
over the bulbs is beneficial. Seeds
can be sown, but take up to seven
years to flower. Normally these
plants are disease- and pest-free.

Take care
Keep moist in dry spells. 36▶

29

Chionodoxa luciliae gigantea
(Glory of the snow)
- **Open sunny site**
- **Ordinary soil**
- **Plant 5-7.5cm (2-3in) deep**

This early-flowering bulb grows to 20cm (8in) tall. The strap-like leaves have blunt tips, and the six-petalled violet-blue flowers with white centres are 4cm (1.6in) across. They are ideal for growing in rock gardens, at the front of beds and in grass; they come into flower in late winter and last until spring.

Plant bulbs 5-7.5cm (2-3in) deep and 7.5-10cm (3-4in) apart in the autumn; for a good effect plant in groups. Lift the plants after several years, divide the bulbs and replant to give more space; the best time is when foliage is dying back. Seeds can be sown in late spring, left for a year and then transplanted into flowering position. Slugs are the worst pest; put down slug bait in the area. Black sooty areas around the flowers are caused by smut; lift and destroy the infected plants, and spray other chionodoxas with Bordeaux mixture.

Take care
Watch for slugs and smut attack. 36♦

Colchicum autumnale
(Autumn crocus)
- **Sun or partial shade**
- **Well-drained soil**
- **Plant 10cm (4in) deep**

This corm produces large mid- to dark green leaves in spring and early summer; these then die back, and from the bare earth spring the stemless flowers in autumn. The leaves grow up to 25cm (10in) long. The flowers are 15cm (6in) long, and from each corm can come several blooms of lilac, rose or white; one variety has double pink flowers.

The corms should be planted in late summer if purchased corms, or from lifted plants when the leaves die down in midsummer. Position them 20cm (8in) apart in clumps, where they can get some sun. Grown from seed, they may take seven years to reach flowering; offsets take only a couple of years to mature. Do not plant too close to smaller plants that may be smothered by the leaves in spring. The area round the corms should be treated to prevent slug attack. Colchicums are normally disease-free.

Take care
Do not let the large leaves smother smaller adjacent plants. 37♦

Colchicum speciosum
(Autumn crocus)
- **Sun or partial shade**
- **Well-drained soil**
- **Plant 10-15cm (4-6in) deep**

This plant flowers in autumn; the flowers are white, rose, purple, violet or crimson, some with coloured veining. Leaves show in spring and last till early summer, 30cm (12in) long and 10cm (4in) wide, four to each bulb.

It is easily cultivated in ordinary well-drained soil, and increases well in grass. Plant a little deeper than *C. autumnale*, in early autumn. Make sure that the leaves do not choke smaller neighbours in spring. Colchicums can be grown from seed, but take up to seven years to reach flowering. Offsets from existing corms will take only two or three years to flower. Lift corms when the leaves have died down in summer, remove the offsets and replant. Keep slugs off with slug bait; the plants are usually disease-free.

Take care
Watch for slug attack on leaves and shoots. 38-9♦

Convallaria majalis
(Lily of the valley)
- **Cool shade**
- **Ordinary soil with leaf-mould**
- **Plant just below the surface**

This plant grows from a creeping horizontal rhizome, and given the right conditions it will spread rapidly. It is spring-flowering, with delicate tiny white or pink scented bells, up to eight bells on a stem. The leaves are in pairs, mid-green and elliptical.

Lilies of the valley grow best in cool moist shade; the soil ought to contain garden compost or leaf-mould to retain moisture. Plant rhizomes in autumn just below the surface, with the pointed end uppermost. Plants can be lifted during late autumn and winter, and divided for replanting. Sow seeds in late summer; they will take up to three years to mature. Grow them first in trays, then move to a nursery bed for two years before transplanting to their final position. Treat the soil with a pesticide to prevent caterpillars; and do not plant this species in wet or boggy areas, as this can cause grey mould.

Take care
Keep the roots moist, but not wet.

Crinum × powellii
- **Warm sheltered site**
- **Rich well-drained soil**
- **Plant up to 30cm (12in) deep**

Crinums are tender, and unless you possess a sheltered border, they are best grown as pot plants. They have mid-green sword-like leaves, and form clumps up to 45cm (18in) tall. The trumpet-like flowers are borne in late summer, 15cm (6in) long, in white or pink or striped with both.

The bulbs should be planted in a warm border in late spring; cover them with ashes, bracken or garden compost to protect from late frosts. If you prefer to grow one as a pot plant, place the bulb in a large pot of rich soil and keep in the greenhouse or indoors until late spring; then it can be moved outside until mid-autumn, when it should be brought indoors again for the winter. Crinums grown from seed can take five years to flower; it is quicker to propagate with offsets from the bulbs, which are removed in spring, potted up and kept moist, and will reach flowering size in three years. They are generally pest- and disease-free.

Take care
Watch for late frosts. 39♦

Crocosmia × crocosmiiflora
(Montbretia)
- **Sunny position**
- **Light sandy soil**
- **Plant 7.5cm (3in) deep**

This well-known plant has sword-like leaves and small but profuse flowers borne on 90cm (36in) stems; the trumpet-shaped blooms, up to 10cm (4in) long, in yellow, orange or deep red, appear throughout the summer.

The plants are hardy and quite invasive. Corms should be planted 7.5cm (3in) deep in a well-drained soil that will retain moisture in the summer, preferably in full sun. The leaves should be cut off in spring before the new growth begins to sprout. Every few years, lift, divide and replant the bulbs with more space around them, just after flowering or in spring. Seeds sown in autumn in pots, and kept in a cold frame, germinate in the spring, and should flower in one or two years. This plant is generally free from pests and diseases.

Take care
Keep this invasive plant under control. 40♦

Above: **Begonia × tuberhybrida**
*An exotic double picotee that will
grow happily out of doors or under
glass as long as the soil is moist and
the air is humid. Keep out of direct
sun by giving light shade.* 24-5♦

Left: **Calochortus venustus**
A simple flower with beautiful markings that tops the delicate tracery of the plant in the summer. Grows well in a dry sandy soil in full sun, or can be grown as a pot plant. 28♦

Right:
Canna × hybrida 'King Humbert'
Justifiably popular for their large leaves, some with a brown to purple colour, and bright blooms that are not unlike those of a gladiolus. 29♦

Below: **Canna × hybrida 'Assault'**
When grouped together in a bed these plants form a fine display, standing over 1m (39in) in height. The flowerheads shine throughout the summer months. 29♦

Above: **Cardiocrinum giganteum**
*A really spectacular plant that towers
above people and is topped with
large trumpets in midsummer. It
needs a rich, well-drained soil and a
lightly shaded location offering
plenty of space.* 29♦

Left:
Chionodoxa luciliae gigantea
*These delicate looking plants bloom
during early spring and will look fine
in the rock garden, borders and in
grass. Thrives in ordinary soil.* 30♦

Right: **Colchicum autumnale**
*An unusual plant that has prolific
leaves in spring and summer. In the
autumn these die back and the
crocus-like blooms spring from the
bare earth, giving a delightful display
when other plants are fading.* 30♦

Above: **Colchicum speciosum**
A corm that blooms after the leaves have died back, producing flowers during the autumn. It enjoys either sun or some shade and brings needed colour to the garden. 31♦

Left:
Colchicum speciosum 'Album'
A white variety that is useful in giving a bright patch in the autumn garden. A low-growing plant that thrives in ordinary soil in either semi-shade or in direct sun. 31♦

Right: **Crinum × powellii**
Invaluable in a sheltered border, where the plant will thrive in a good, well-drained soil. Produces the fine trumpet like blooms in late summer. Can also be grown as a pot plant. 32♦

Above: **Crocosmia ×
crocosmiiflora 'Emily McKenzie'**
*Commonly known as montbretia,
this is one of the many large-
flowered varieties available.* 32▸

Left:
Crocus aureus 'Dutch Yellow'
*Fine for rock and sink gardens as
well as for borders and growing in
grass. Provides spring colour.* 49▸

Right: **Crocosmia masonorum**
*This plant gives a continuous display
of blooms throughout the summer,
provided it has plenty of sun and the
soil is not too moist.* 49▸

Above: **Crocus tomasinianus**
One of the first crocuses to flower, it produces blooms in late winter. The plant needs some protection to give it a good start but will then thrive in most areas of the garden. 50♦

Left:
Crocus chrysanthus 'Blue Bird'
This crocus shows a blue bud that opens out to reveal the creamy-white inside with a deep orange centre. It will thrive in full sun in any well-drained soil. 50♦

Right:
Crocus vernus 'Striped Beauty'
A large-flowering crocus with very delicate veining on the petals. The plant will increase naturally if the soil is free-draining and sunny. 51♦

43

Left: Cyclamen hederifolium
Shade-loving plants that enjoy a woodland situation, where they will spread naturally. They flower from midsummer until late autumn, providing well needed colour at ground level under the trees. 52▸

Right: Dahlia 'Claire de Lune' (Anemone-flowered)
Often growing to over 1m (39in) in height, these dahlias will flower all summer until the late autumn frosts. Ideal for the back of the border. 53▸

Below: Dahlia 'Scarlet Comet' (Anemone-flowered)
These are grown for their brilliant colours and spectacular blooms with an inner ring of petals that surround the centre like a halo. Highly suited to the border where colour is needed. 53▸

Above: **Dahlia 'Geerling's Elite' (Collarette)**
Brilliantly coloured blooms to grace any border, each with a small collar of petals around the centre. These are very free-flowering plants. 54♦

Above: Dahlia 'Bishop of Llandaff' (Paeony-flowered)
These blooms have rings of flat petals surrounding the central core of stamens. Fine border plants. 54♦

Below: Dahlia 'Yma Sumac' (Decorative)
These dahlias are recognised by the double blooms with the petals often twisted. Wide choice of sizes. 55♦

Above: **Dahlia 'Vicky Jackson' (Decorative)**
A beautiful bloom that would grace any garden. Decorative dahlias are available in delicate shades and are free-flowering from midsummer until the frosts of late autumn. The blooms can vary from 10cm (4in) to 25cm (10in) across. 55♦

Left: **Dahlia 'Schwieter's Kokarde' (Decorative)**
Decorative dahlias can reach up to 150cm (5ft) tall, with flowers in proportion to suit most borders and beds. The taller varieties should be staked against wind damage. 55♦

Crocosmia masonorum

- Sunny place
- Well-drained sandy soil
- Plant 7.5cm (3in) deep

This South African plant has sword-like leaves with pronounced centre spines, and grows to 75cm (30in) tall. The flowers are bright orange, 2.5cm (1in) long, and the plant will give a succession of blooms from midsummer.

These plants can be invasive; confine them by planting in a bottomless container sunk into the ground. The corms should be planted in spring, 7.5cm (3in) deep and 15cm (6in) apart, in a sunny position. The plants need a well-drained soil, but keep it moist during summer droughts. The flowers are often used for cutting; if they are left on the plants, remove them as soon as they die. Cut off dead leaves before the new ones appear in spring. Corms should be lifted every few years; divide after flowering and before new growth appears. They are normally pest- and disease-free.

Take care
Stop plants spreading too far. 41▶

Crocus aureus 'Dutch Yellow'

- Sunny position
- Well-drained soil
- Plant 7.5cm (3in) deep – more in a light soil

The yellow flowering crocus has fine grass-like leaves, and produces its bright blooms in early spring, growing to 10cm (4in) long. It prefers well-drained soil and a sunny situation, and is recommended for rock gardens. It also thrives in short grass, provided no mowing occurs before the leaves turn yellow in late spring.

Corms should be planted in autumn to flower the following spring, in groups or drifts; plant them 7.5cm (3in) apart. Crocuses multiply by cormlets produced around the parent corm, or by seeding. Cormlets can be removed in early summer and grown on to flower in two years' time; seed takes up to four years to flower, and should be sown in summer and transplanted into nursery beds when large enough to handle. A general pesticide will keep most trouble at bay. Also use a fungicide.

Take care
Bird attack can be averted by black cotton stretched over the plants. 40▶

Crocus chrysanthus 'Blue Bird'

- Sheltered sunny position
- Well-drained soil
- Plant 7.5cm (3in) deep

This spring-flowering crocus has a bloom with a mauve-blue exterior edged with white, a creamy white inside and a deep orange centre, and it flowers profusely. The short narrow leaves of pale green have a paler stripe along the spine.

These crocuses are ideal for the border or rockery, and do well in pots in a cold greenhouse. Corms can be planted in any free-draining soil. If the soil is very light, they can be planted 15cm (6in) deep, but otherwise 7.5cm (3in) is recommended. If crocuses are grown in grass, delay mowing until the leaves turn yellow and die back; if you cut sooner, the corms will produce very poor blooms next season. Treat the soil with a general pesticide and fungicide. Mice and birds can be deterred by the use of mouse bait and black cotton stretched over the plants; but a cat is as good a deterrent as any.

Take care
Keep the corms from becoming waterlogged. 42♦

Crocus tomasinianus

- Sunny site sheltered against cold winds
- Ordinary well-drained soil
- Plant 7.5cm (3in) deep

This winter-flowering crocus has smaller flowers than the spring crocus, up to 7.5cm (3in) long. The delicate blue-lavender flowers bud in winter and open in very early spring. They naturalize well in grass and sunny borders, given a sheltered position, and do well also in groups under deciduous trees or on rockeries. The varieties available are mostly deep purples such as 'Bar's Purple' and 'Whitewell Purple', but a white variety called 'Albus' is for sale from some specialists.

Corms should be planted 7.5cm (3in) deep, but if the soil is very light and summer cultivation is likely to disturb the roots, they can be planted as deep as 15cm (6in). Do not remove flowers as they die, and leave foliage until it can be pulled off. Increase stock by growing the cormlets, which should flower in two years. Treat soil with a pesticide and fungicide.

Take care
Leave flowers and leaves on the plant until leaves turn yellow. 42-3♦

Crocus vernus 'Striped Beauty'
- Sheltered but sunny place
- Well-drained soil
- Plant 7.5cm (3in) deep

Curtonus paniculatus
- Sheltered border
- Well-drained soil with plenty of humus
- Plant 15cm (6in) deep

C. vernus is the parent of the large Dutch crocuses, which over several centuries have resulted in blooms of great variety, up to 12.5cm (5in) long. 'Striped Beauty' has a large flower of silver white with dark purple-blue stripes and a violet-purple base to the petals.

Corms should be planted 7.5cm (3in) deep, or more if the soil is light and sandy, and not less than 10cm (4in) apart. Over the years the corms will multiply naturally to form dense mats of flowers, which are spectacular in grass under deciduous trees. The grass-like leaves should pull off easily when they turn yellow after flowering. At this time the corms can be lifted and divided; remove the cormlets and keep in a nursery area, where they will mature in two years. Treat the soil with a general pesticide and fungicide.

Take care
Do not dead-head or cut leaves until the leaves die back. 43♦

This plant is sometimes classified as *Antholyza* or *Tritonia*; it is closely related to crocosmias, freesias, ixias and sparaxis. It is hardy, and in the herbaceous border it will grow to 120cm (4ft); in ideal conditions it may reach 150cm (5ft). The sword-like leaves are up to 75cm (30in) long. In late summer the plant produces a succession of blooms on tall branching stems; at each division it bears an orange-red trumpet-shaped flower, 5cm (2in) long.

Corms should be planted 15cm (6in) deep in autumn, in a well-drained soil containing fibrous material. The position should be warm and protected against frost until it is established, when it will be hardy. When flowers die back in autumn, the stems should be cut. At this time the plants can be lifted and divided, but keep them moist until growth starts. This species is generally pest- and disease-free.

Take care
Protect from frost until established.

Cyclamen hederifolium
- Shade
- Soil with added leaf-mould
- Plant just under the surface

This Mediterranean plant is hardy and will grow in poor soil, but it thrives if covered with a 2.5cm (1in) layer of leaf-mould in late spring, after the leaves have died down. The plant grows to only 10cm (4in), often much less. The silvery leaves have dark green markings on the upper surface, and underneath they are red.

Plant the corms 10-15cm (4-6in) apart in a light soil that has plenty of leaf-mould in it; they will thrive in woodland if left undisturbed. Grow cyclamen from seed: sow in pots or trays in late summer and leave the container outside on its side to prevent it becoming waterlogged. Germination will occur the following spring, and seedlings can be potted on, planting out when they are large enough to handle easily, in either late spring or late summer. Treat with a general pesticide; disease is mainly due to wet conditions, so treat the area also with a fungicide.

Take care
Ensure that the soil is well-drained and not waterlogged. 44▸

Cyclamen persicum
- Sheltered and shady situation
- Well-drained soil with plenty of humus
- Plant 5cm (2in) deep

This cyclamen group is much larger than *C. hederifolium.* The original variety is parent to a wide range of plants, forming two main groups: first, the less hardy garden cyclamen, with flowers up to 6.5cm (2.6in) long, in colours ranging from white through pinks and reds to purple, and some with decorative leaf markings; and second, the tender, florists' pot plants with even larger blooms, some of which are scented.

The outdoor varieties grow well in sheltered areas out of direct sun. If you are growing the pot varieties use a soil mixture that has plenty of leaf-mould or peat. Keep the pots cool, moist and shaded from hot sun, keep at 13-16°C (55-60°F) and place in full light. If the air is dried by central heating, keep cyclamen moist. The plants will bloom through the winter, and can be rested during summer. Use a general pesticide and fungicide.

Take care
Avoid watering the centre of the cyclamen.

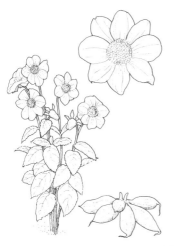 

Dahlia
(Single-flowered)

- Open sunny site
- Rich well-drained soil
- Plant 10cm (4in) deep

These half-hardy tuberous plants are popular as border specimens. They come into flower in summer and continue until the first frost. The single-flowered varieties have blooms up to 10cm (4in) across, in red, lilac or pink, and consist of a single row of petals around a central disc of stamens. The plants grow up to 75cm (30in) tall.

Plant the tubers outdoors in mid-spring, but if they are already sprouting keep them in a frost-free place until late spring, when they can be planted out. A rich, well-drained soil is needed, with fertilizer or manure added before planting. Place in an open and sunny situation and give the growing plant some support. Remove dead flowers and pinch out leading shoots to encourage larger blooms. Tubers should be lifted and stored each autumn. Spray with a general pesticide and fungicide. If the leaves turn yellow and wilt, destroy the plant to stop the virus.

Take care
Protect young shoots from cold winds and late frosts.

Dahlia
(Anemone-flowered)

- Open sunny site
- Rich well-drained soil
- Plant 10cm (4in) deep

This variety will grow to 105cm (42in), with blooms some 10cm (4in) in diameter. The flowers are double, with the outer petals flat and the inner ones tubular and much shorter, often in contrasting colours. Blooms appear in summer and continue through to the autumn frosts, giving a brilliant show of red, purple, yellow or white.

Tubers can be started in the warmth but must not be planted out until the danger of frosts has passed. Unsprouted tubers can be planted in late spring; the shoots will not pierce the surface until the frosts have gone. The soil should have plenty of organic material added to it, to feed the roots and to retain moisture during dry periods. Remove dead flowers. Lift the plant in autumn and store the tubers in a frost-free place during winter. Spray with a pesticide and fungicide. If leaves turn yellow and wilt, destroy the plant to prevent spread of virus.

Take care
Keep tubers moist in droughts. 44-5▶

Dahlia (Collarette)
- **Sunny sheltered place**
- **Rich and moist but well-drained soil**
- **Plant 10cm (4in) deep**

This half-hardy plant will grow to 120cm (4ft) tall, with a spread of 75cm (30in). The leaves are bright green and make a good foil for the blooms, which are up to 10cm (4in) across in white, yellow, orange, red or pink. The flowers have an outer ring of flat petals with an inner collar of smaller petals around the central disc of stamens. Blooms appear from late summer to the frosts in autumn, when the plant should be lifted and the tuber stored.

The following spring they can be started off in the greenhouse, and the sprouting plant put out in late spring; or the unsprouted tuber can be put out in mid-spring. The soil should be rich in organic material, compost, bonemeal or manure. Plant in full sun; shelter plants from wind or support the dahlia with a stake. Spray with a general pesticide and fungicide. Destroy plants if the leaves wilt and turn yellow.

Take care
Protect against frost both when growing and in store. 46♦

Dahlia (Paeony-flowered)
- **Open sunny site**
- **Rich well-drained soil**
- **Plant 10cm (4in) deep**

This dahlia is descended from Mexican species, and grows to 90cm (36in) tall, with a spread of 60cm (24in). The flowers, 10cm (4in) across, consist of an outer ring of flat petals and one or more inner rings of flat petals around a central core of stamens, in orange, red or purple. Plant the tubers 10cm (4in) deep in well-drained soil with plenty of organic material mixed in to supply nutrients and retain moisture. This border plant should be grown with other dahlias for best effect. The flowers start in late summer and continue until the late autumn frosts.

The tuber should then be lifted and stored free from frost until the following year, when it can be planted out in spring. Alternatively, keep the tuber in a greenhouse to encourage early sprouting, but then it should not be planted out until late spring. Spray with a pesticide and fungicide. If the leaves turn yellow and the plant wilts, destroy it.

Take care
Do not damage the growing points on the tuber. 47♦

Dahlia (Decorative)
● Open sunny position
● Rich well-drained soil
● Plant 10cm (4in) deep

Dahlia (Ball)
● Open sunny place
● Rich well-drained soil
● Plant 10cm (4in) deep

This group of dahlias is distinguished by the truly double blooms of flat petals, often twisted and normally with blunt points. The group divides into five sections: giant, large, medium, small and miniature. The giants grow to 150cm (5ft), with blooms up to 25cm (10in) across; the miniatures have a height of 90cm (3ft), with flowers 10cm (4in) in diameter. The colours include white, yellow, orange, red, pink, purple and lavender, with some multicolours.

They all flower from late summer until the autumn frosts. Then the plants should be lifted and the tubers stored in a frost-free place until spring. Support plants with stakes, particularly the taller varieties, which are more prone to wind damage. Remove all but one bud from each stem to encourage larger blooms. Remove dead flowers to ensure further flowering. Treat the plants with a pesticide and fungicide.

This group is noted for the ball-shaped blooms. They are fully double; the petals appear to be tubular and open out at the blunt end, and they are arranged in a spiral. The group is split into two sections: the standard ball has blooms over 10cm (4in) in diameter; and the miniature ball has blooms under 10cm (4in). Both will grow to 120cm (4ft) tall, and spread 75cm (30in). The colours include white, yellow, orange, red, mauve and purple.

Plant tubers in a well-drained soil rich in organic material, in an area that is open to the sun but sheltered from the wind; mature plants should be staked to prevent wind damage. Sprouted tubers should not be planted in the open until danger of frost has passed, unsprouted ones can be planted out in spring. Spray plants with a pesticide and fungicide. Wilting plants with yellow leaves must be destroyed at once.

Take care
Inspect tubers in winter, and destroy diseased or damaged ones. 47, 48♦

Take care
Stake plants to keep wind damage to a minimum. 65♦

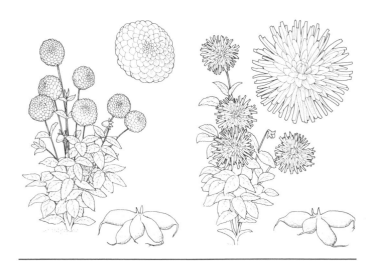

Dahlia (Pompon)
- **Open sunny site**
- **Well-drained rich soil**
- **Plant 10cm (4in) deep**

These plants are similar to the ball dahlias but their blooms are only 5cm (2in) in diameter, the shape is more ball-like, and the petals are tubular for their whole length. They flower in late summer and continue to the first frosts; colours include lilac, red, purple and white. They grow to 120cm (4ft) tall, and 75cm (30in) across.

Plant in a section of the garden that is open but sheltered from the wind. The tubers, if unsprouted, can be planted in mid-spring, but sprouted tubers should be kept in the greenhouse until late spring. Give the plants some support and pinch out the leading shoots one month after planting. When the plants are cut down by frosts, lift and store the tubers in a frost-free place until the following spring. Plants should be treated with a pesticide and fungicide; wilting dahlias with yellow leaves should be destroyed.

Take care
Keep soil moist in droughts.

Dahlia (Cactus)
- **Open sunny site**
- **Rich well-drained soil**
- **Plant 10cm (4in) deep**

This group of dahlias can be divided into five sections: miniature, small, medium, large and giant. They are exotic, with the petals rolled back or quilled for over half their length; the largest flowers reach 25cm (10in) in diameter, but the smallest are only 10cm (4in). The colours include white, yellow, orange, red and purple, with some delicate shades of pink and lilac. The larger plants grow to 150cm (5ft) tall and almost 120cm (4ft) across; the smaller ones are 90cm (36in) tall and 75cm (30in) across.

Tubers should preferably be planted in open sun, but will stand some shade. Plant them outdoors in mid-spring or start them off in a greenhouse and plant out in late spring. Spray with a pesticide and fungicide; wilting plants with yellow leaves should be destroyed.

Take care
Winter storage of tubers must be frost-free. 66◗

Dahlia (Semi-cactus)
- **Open but sheltered site**
- **Well-drained rich soil**
- **Plant 10cm (4in) deep**

Very closely related to the cactus dahlia, the semi-cactus has broader petals that are not tubular or quilled for half their length. Sizes are the same, ranging from 10-25cm (4-10in). The plants have the same bright green leaves and range of flower colour, but the spikiness is less distinct and some have fluted ends to the petals.

Plant in a good well-drained soil rich in humus, and in sunshine, though if necessary they can stand partial shade. The tubers should be planted 10cm (4in) deep in spring, provided they have not started sprouting; otherwise keep them in a frost-free place until late spring, when frosts are over. Provide some support to prevent wind damage. After flowering, remove the dead heads to encourage further flowers. When frost has cut down the dahlias, lift and store the tubers. Spray with a pesticide and fungicide.

Take care
Keep tubers from standing in waterlogged soil. 67, 68♦

Dahlia (Bedding)
- **Open sunny site**
- **Well-drained rich soil**
- **Plant 5-10cm (2-4in) deep**

These small dahlias are normally grown from seed and treated like annuals. They grow 30-50cm (12-20in) tall with a similar spread. The leaves are bright green; flowers can be single, semi-double or double, in colours from white through yellows and reds to lilac, and 5-7.5cm (2-3in) in diameter. They start to bloom in midsummer and continue until the autumn frosts.

After the first year, when they are grown from seed, tubers are formed and can be lifted and kept in a frost-free place during winter. If tubers shrivel, soak them in water overnight and then dry them before putting them back into storage. They can be planted the following year in spring unless they have started to sprout, in which case keep them in moist peat until late spring, when they can be planted outside. Seed can be sown in late winter at a temperature of 16°C (60°F), transplanted when large enough to handle, and planted out in late spring in the flowering position. Spray with a pesticide and fungicide.

Take care
Cover plants if frost is forecast. 69♦

Dierama pulcherrimum

(Wandflower)
- **Sunny sheltered site**
- **Ordinary well-drained soil**
- **Plant 10-15cm (4-6in) deep**

This cormous plant is hardy except in the coldest areas. It grows to 180cm (6ft) tall, with grass-like leaves reaching 90cm (36in) in length. The trumpet-shaped hanging flowers, on arching stems, are often 2.5cm (1in) long, and the spread of the plant will reach 60cm (24in). The flowers, in red, violet, purple or white, appear in late summer and last until autumn.

Plant the corms in well-drained soil; there should be at least 10cm (4in) of soil over the corm, and preferably 15cm (6in). Plant in either spring or autumn, and leave undisturbed. If plants become overcrowded they can be lifted in autumn, divided and replanted. In cold areas, lift the corms in autumn and store until spring. Offsets can be removed from the corms in autumn, and will reach flowering in 18 months. Seed can be sown and takes up to three years to flower. Normally plants are pest- and disease-free.

Take care
Leave plants undisturbed.

Endymion hispanicus

- **Open or lightly shade position**
- **Moist but not boggy soil**
- **Plant 10-15cm (4-6in) deep**

This plant was included in the genus *Scilla* but now has its own genus. It grows to a height of 30cm (12in), with broad strap-like leaves, and bell-shaped white, blue or pink flowers from spring to midsummer. It thrives on neglect and is ideal for growing in the open.

Bulbs should be planted 10-15cm (4-6in) deep, in a moist soil with plenty of organic matter. The bulbs have no outer skin, and should be out of the soil as little as possible. Do not store bulbs, as they shrivel when dry or go mouldy if too wet.

Propagate by lifting the bulbs and removing offsets, which can then be replanted with more space around them. Seed sown on leaf-mould may take six years to flower. Yellow spots that turn to dark brown blotches indicate rust; remove and destroy infected leaves, and spray with zineb.

Take care
Avoid waterlogged soil. 69♦

Endymion non-scriptus
(English bluebell)
- Open sun or light shade
- Moist but not waterlogged soil
- Plant 10-15cm (4-6in) deep

This bulbous plant, widespread throughout Western Europe, gives spectacular shows of blue in light woodland and open ground. In Scotland, it is called the wild hyacinth. The strap-like leaves are a glossy mid-green; the purple-blue, white or pink bell-shaped flowers appear in spring. The plant grows to 30cm (12in), and has a spread of 10cm (4in), although the mature leaves will spread further as they become less erect.

The bulbs should be planted 10-15cm (4-6in) deep. They have no outer skin, so the less time they spend out of soil the better. Choose a moist soil with plenty of leaf-mould in it. Plants are increased by lifting and dividing the bulbs after the foliage has died down in autumn. Seed can take up to six years to flower. Endymions are normally pest- and disease-free.

Take care
Replant bulbs quickly, and handle as little as possible.

Eranthis hyemalis
(Winter aconite)
- Sun or partial shade
- Well-drained heavy soil
- Plant 2.5cm (1in) deep

This European tuberous-rooted plant grows to a height of 10cm (4in) with a spread of 7.5cm (3in). The leaves are pale green and deeply cut, and the bright yellow flowers appear in late winter; in mild winters it may start blooming in midwinter. The flowers are about 2.5cm (1in) across and look like buttercups but with a collar of pale green leaves just below the flower.

Plant tubers in a well-drained soil that is moist throughout the year – a heavy loam is ideal. Grow them in either sun or light shade. To propagate, lift the eranthis when the leaves die down, break or cut the tubers into sections, and replant these immediately, at least 7.5cm (3in) apart. Seed can be sown in spring and kept in a cold frame; transplant in two years, and flowering will start after another year. Watch for bird attack. If sooty eruptions occur on the plant, destroy it to stop the spread of smut disease.

Take care
Keep soil moist in spring. 70-71▶

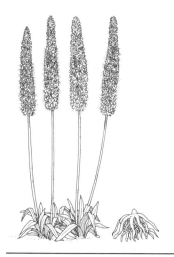 

Eremurus robustus
(Foxtail lily)
- **Sunny sheltered border**
- **Well-drained soil**
- **Plant 1.25cm (0.5in) deep**

This dramatic plant reaches 3m (10ft) high, with bright sword-like leaves 120cm (4ft) in length. The flowers, which have the appearance of bushy foxtails, are 120cm (4ft) spikes of star-like blooms, peach-buff to pink in colour. They appear in summer.

The plants should be kept in a sheltered border, with an aspect to catch midday to evening sun, and the soil should be well-drained with plenty of fibre. The crown of the tuber should have only 1.25cm (0.5in) of soil over it, although some growers recommend planting as deep as 15cm (6in) in light soils. Leave undisturbed until tubers become crowded, then lift, divide and replant in autumn. The flower stems should be cut down when blooming stops, unless seed is needed. Spread well-rotted manure or compost over the area in autumn. Seeds are slow to germinate and take several years to reach flowering size.

Take care
Not suitable for windy sites.

Erythronium dens-canis
(Dog's tooth violet)
- **Semi-shade**
- **Moist well-drained soil**
- **Plant 7.5cm (3in) deep**

This cormous plant grows only 15cm (6in) tall. The spotted leaves vary from plant to plant, and some are particularly attractive. The 5cm (2in) flowers appear in spring and the petals are folded back like a cyclamen; they are available in white, pink, red and violet, each flower having a pair of leaves up to 10cm (4in) long.

Corms should be planted in autumn, preferably in groups of at least a dozen for show, in a moist but well-drained soil; choose a partially shaded site. Here they can be left for many years undisturbed. Increasing stock by growing from seed can take over five years to reach flowering size. It is quicker to remove offsets in late summer, when the leaves have died down, and to grow them separately in a nursery bed for a year or so; they should take two years to start flowering, and then they can be planted out in autumn. Generally pest- and disease-free.

Take care
Keep these plants moist. 70♦

Erythronium tuolumnense

- Shady situation
- Moist but not waterlogged soil
- Plant 10cm (4in) deep

This plant grows to 30cm (12in), with a spread of 15cm (6in). It has bright green leaves that are broad and pointed. The spring flowers have six pointed yellow petals and are rather like small lilies.

The corms should be planted 10cm (4in) deep, in a moist but not boggy soil that has plenty of leaf-mould to keep it well-drained, and with some shade. They should be planted in late summer and can be left undisturbed until they become overcrowded; then lift, divide and replant when the leaves die down in summer. Seed takes over five years to reach flowering; it is quicker to increase stock from offsets, which reach flowering in three years. Make sure the soil does not dry out when plants are young, as they need constantly moist soil to thrive. A good layer of well-rotted manure or compost spread over the plants in autumn keeps the organic level high.

Take care
Keep the soil moist (but not wet) until plants are established. 71♦

Eucomis bicolor

(Pineapple flower)
- Open position or light shade
- Rich well-drained soil
- Plant 2.5cm (1in) deep

This plant reaches 70cm (28in) tall, with a spread of 45cm (18in). It has long broad strap-like leaves with pronounced centre spines, and cream flowers in summer borne on fleshy stems crowned with rosettes of petal-like leaves.

It thrives in a rich well-drained soil with plenty of leaf-mould in it. This plant is hardy and needs only a mulch of well-rotted manure each autumn to protect it from hard frosts in winter. Bulbs can be lifted in very early spring, and the offsets separated and replanted; the parent bulbs then have more space to grow, and offsets reach flowering size in two or three years provided they are kept moist all summer and shaded from the sun.

If this species is grown as a pot plant, it should be kept moist in summer but the pot should be rested on its side during winter to allow the soil to dry out. Grown from seed it takes several years to flower.

Take care
Protect from hard frosts.

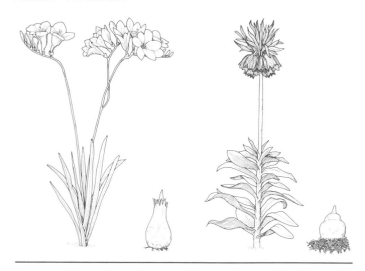

Freesia × hybrida
- **Sheltered sunny situation**
- **Light sandy soil**
- **Plant 5cm (2in) deep**

These plants grow to 45cm (18in) tall, with a spread of 15cm (6in). The leaves are narrow and sword-like, and the flower stems have spikes of scented trumpet-shaped 5cm (2in) blooms in summer. Although most are suitable for the greenhouse only, some are available for growing out of doors, being planted in spring to flower in the summer of the first season only. A wide variety of exquisite colours is available, from white through yellow to pink, red, magenta and violet.

Freesias need a light sandy soil and a position that is sunny and sheltered from cold winds. Plant the corms in spring unless you have a frost-free area, where they can be planted in late summer to flower the following spring. After flowering the corms can be lifted and treated as greenhouse bulbs where they can provide flowers in early spring, but they need a minimum temperature of 5°C (41°F). Offsets removed in late summer flower the following year.

Take care
Protect from frost. 72▶

Fritillaria imperialis
(Crown imperial)
- **Full or partial shade**
- **Well-drained soil**
- **Plant 20cm (8in) deep**

This plant grows up to 90cm (36in) tall, with a centre stem on which is carried a series of narrow pointed glossy leaves to half the total height; the top half of this stem carries a circle of large beautiful drooping flowers about 5cm (2in) long, which is topped with a green crown of leaves. The range of bloom colour is yellow, orange and red.

The bulb should be planted in autumn in a rich well-drained soil in shade, preferably where it can be left undisturbed. Handle bulbs carefully and do not let them dry out. Plant the bulb on its side to stop water getting into the hollow crown and rotting the bulb. In heavy soil a handful of coarse sand around the bulb will speed drainage. Cut the stems down when they die off in summer. Seed will not produce flowering bulbs for six years. It is quicker to use offsets taken from the parent bulb in late summer; plant them out in a nursery bed for two years, then transplant them to the flowering position.

Take care
Do not bruise or dry the bulb. 73▶

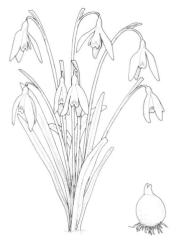

Fritillaria meleagris
(Snake's head fritillary)
- Full or semi-shade
- Well-drained fertile soil
- Plant 15cm (6in) deep

These fritillarias have delicate blooms with a fine chequerboard pattern. They grow to 45cm (18in) tall with fine grass-like leaves mid- to blue-green in colour. The blooms are just under 5cm (2in) in length and hang down like bells, appearing in spring. The flowers are purple, brown, violet-red and white; the white varieties do not have the chequerboard pattern, but some have fine green veining instead.

They should be planted in the autumn, 15cm (6in) deep on their side, in rich fertile soil that is well-drained, and in full or partial shade. Leave undisturbed for at least four years; then they can be lifted, and the bulblets removed and replanted in a nursery bed for two years, then transplanted to their final flowering positions. When young, they should be kept moist but not wet; if the soil is too wet, mix in plenty of sharp sand to aid drainage. Fritillarias are generally pest- and disease-free.

Take care
Avoid waterlogged sites.

Galanthus nivalis
(Snowdrop)
- Partial shade
- Rich well-drained soil
- Plant 10-15cm (4-6in) deep

Snowdrop leaves are flat, sword-shaped and often blue-green in colour. The flowers are either single or double, in white with green markings on the inner petals, and can be as long as 2.5cm (1in). Snowdrops' time of flowering depends on the severity or mildness of the winter weather, but normally starts around midwinter. One variety flowers in late autumn, before the leaves appear. They can grow up to 20cm (8in) tall in rich soil and in partial shade.

The bulbs should be planted 10cm (4in) deep in heavy soil, or 15cm (6in) deep in light soil, in autumn; the soil should be moist but well-drained. Move bulbs after they have finished flowering, while the soil is moist. Seed may take five years to bloom, so it is better to split clusters of bulbs and spread them out. Take care when lifting not to damage the roots or to let them dry out. Use a soil insecticide and fungicide.

Take care
Leave bulbs undisturbed for several years for improved flowering. 74-5♦

63

Galtonia candicans
(Summer hyacinth)
- Full sun
- Moist well-drained soil
- Plant 15cm (6in) deep

This plant grows up to 120cm (4ft),
with narrow sword-like pointed
leaves 75cm (30in) long. The dozen
or so scented flowers appear in late
summer on a single stem; they are
bell-shaped, almost 5cm (2in) long,
and white in colour with green
markings at the tip and base of the
petals.

The large round bulbs should be
grouped and planted in spring in a
rich well-drained soil. They are hardy
in the more temperate areas but
where there are hard frosts it is better
to treat galtonias as pot plants. As pot
plants they should be started in
autumn in order to flower late the
following spring, but keep them at a
temperature of not less than 4°C
(39°F) for success. Seed takes up to
five years to flower; but offsets taken
in autumn will flower in two years.
Treat the soil with slug bait around
the plants, and spray with fungicide
to keep grey mould to a minimum,
especially with newly planted bulbs.

Take care
Protect from severe frost by covering
with bracken or a thick mulch.74♦

Gladiolus byzantinus
- Full sun
- Ordinary rich garden soil
- Plant 10cm (4in) deep

This hardy plant, up to 60cm (24in)
tall, has a flower spike about 40cm
(16in) long. A succession of wine-
red blooms, 5-7.5cm (2-3in) across,
appear along the spike in
midsummer. The leaves are sword-
shaped with pointed tips.

Plant in full sun in ordinary garden
soil fed with manure, in either
autumn or spring. Plant a little deeper
in light soil, to give more anchorage.
In heavy soil a base of sharp sand
under the corm will help drainage
and prevent rot. Keep the young
plants weeded, and after 10 weeks of
growth start watering well. In the
autumn the leaves will die back;
remove them when they virtually fall
off. After a few years lift them and
remove the cormlets to increase the
stock; these take up to three years to
flower. Treat the plant with a
pesticide and fungicide to prevent
trouble. If a plant looks sick and turns
yellow, destroy it to stop the virus
spreading.

Take care
Avoid waterlogged soil. 75♦

Above: **Dahlia 'Kay Helen' (Ball)**
A very neat and compact bloom that will look equally splendid in either the garden border or as a cut flower indoors. Dahlias will thrive in a rich soil and a sunny position. 55♦

Above: **Dahlia 'Match' (Cactus)**
A lovely example of a multicoloured bloom, with its spiky double flowers and the petals rolled or quilled. 56♦

Below: **Dahlia 'Salmon Keene' (Cactus)**
One of the more regular shaped blooms of this group. 56♦

Above: **Dahlia 'Earl Marc'**
(Semi-cactus)
Not as quilled or tubular as the cactus, this bloom has flatter petals. Semi-cactus flowers can reach 25cm (10in) across. 57▶

Left: **Dahlia 'Primrose Bryn' (Semi-cactus)**
These sun-loving plants thrive in an open border with rich garden soil. The blooms continue throughout the summer until late autumn. 57♦

Right: **Dahlia 'Gypsy Dance' (Bedding)**
Ideal for the front of borders and in bedding arrangements. The small brightly coloured flowers come in single and double forms. 57♦

Below: **Endymion hispanicus**
Often referred to as the Spanish bluebell, this plant enjoys a moist soil and thrives on neglect. It will grow in either the open or in the light shade of woodland. 58♦

Left: Erythronium dens-canis
A low-growing plant that has beautifully marked leaves and delicate blooms that appear in the spring and often continue until summer. Provide some shade. 60♦

Right: Erythronium tuolumnense
This plant loves a moist soil and shade, where it will flower in spring with yellow lily-like blooms. It likes to be left alone and undisturbed; a woodland site is ideal. 61♦

Below: Eranthis hyemalis
A ground-hugging plant with brilliant yellow flowers that look like buttercups and appear in midwinter if conditions are mild. It thrives in a heavy soil that is moist throughout the year. 59♦

Left: **Freesia 'Prince of Orange'**
A fine form of this perfumed flower that needs plenty of sun and shelter from the cold. It will thrive in a light sandy soil and bloom during the midsummer months. 62♦

Right: **Fritillaria imperialis**
A most unusual and impressive plant with drooping flowers and a crown of leaves on a tall stem. It needs a shady or partially shady situation and a well-drained soil to thrive. 62♦

Below: **Freesia 'Red Star'**
Although normally grown under glass, some varieties are available for outdoor use. All have highly coloured and scented flowers and sword-like leaves. Plant corms in spring. 62♦

Left: **Galtonia candicans**
In full sun and a moist soil, this plant will reward the grower with scented blooms throughout the summer. Reaching over 1m (39in) in height, the galtonia is suited to the back of the border. 64♦

Right: **Gladiolus byzantinus**
A small-flowered gladiolus that blooms much earlier than its large-flowered relations and does not need staking. Place in full sun in groups to make the most of the flowers. 64♦

Below: **Galanthus nivalis**
Normally flowering in midwinter, the low-growing snowdrop is often regarded as the herald of spring. It will grow best in light shade and a good soil that is moist and free-draining. Handle bulbs with care. 63♦

75

Above: **Gladiolus 'Spring Green'**
*A small summer-flowering
primulinus gladiolus with a slender
and graceful form that is fine for cut
flowers as well as the border.* 81♦

Left: **Gladiolus 'Nanus Minetto'**
*A miniature hybrid gladiolus with
delicate form and finely marked
blooms. These look well in flower
arrangements and also in the garden
border, ideally near the front.* 82♦

Right: **Gladiolus 'Aristocrat'**
*One of the large-flowered varieties
available in brilliant colours. By
staggering the planting you can have
blooms throughout the summer.* 81♦

Above:
Ipheion uniflorum 'Violaceum'
These spring-flowering plants have star-shaped scented blooms. 86♦

Far left: **Hyacinthus orientalis 'Anna Marie'**
These indoor bulbs are treated for forcing to give blooms in winter. 84♦

Left:
Hyacinthus orientalis 'Ostara'
A spring garden variety that will look good singly or en masse. 85♦

Right: **Hymenocallis × festalis**
A scented summer-flowering plant that has a narcissus-like trumpet and long slender petals. 85♦

Above: **Iris pumila 'Green Spot'
(Pogoniris/Eupogon)**
A bearded iris with fine markings that
thrives in a sunny border and blooms
in early summer, after spring bulbs
and before the summer flowers. 87►

Gladiolus (Large-flowered)

- Full sun
- Ordinary garden soil with added humus
- Plant 10-15cm (4-6in) deep

The large-flowered gladiolus hybrids are half-hardy plants that need some protection against frost. The plants often reach 120cm (4ft) high. The flower spike is about 50cm (20in) long, and individual blooms are 17.5cm (7in) across. They flower in summer, in vivid shades of white, yellow, orange, red, purple, rust, pink and mauve, either with markings or plain.

These hybrids are easily grown from corms planted 10-15cm (4-6in) deep; in lighter soils plant at the greater depth. Put some sharp sand under the corms to aid drainage, and place in full sun. An ordinary garden soil with some manure added is ideal. As they mature, the plants may become top-heavy, so staking is useful. When the plant dies back after flowering, lift it and store the new corm in a frost-free place for the following year. Treat with pesticide and fungicide to keep plants healthy.

Take care
Protect against frost and excessive wetness. 77♦

Gladiolus (Primulinus hybrids)

- Full sun
- Ordinary garden soil enriched with manure
- Plant 10-15cm (4-6in) deep

These are not as vigorous or as big as the large-flowered gladiolus but they are free-flowering and decorative. The plants grow to a height of 45-90cm (18-36in), with the flower spike almost 40cm (16in) long; the flowers themselves, up to 7.5cm (3in) across, are placed alternately on the stem, and bloom after midsummer. A variety of colours is available, some with stripes and contrasting throats. The leaves are long, slender and sword-shaped.

The plant is half-hardy, surviving in some winters underground, but normally the corm is lifted in autumn. A new corm is found above the old one, which is discarded; store the young corm in a frost-free place during the winter. Grow in a well-drained soil, keeping it moist in the summer at flowering time. Treat with a fungicide to keep rot and fungus at bay.

Take care
Destroy diseased corms to prevent spread. 76♦

Gladiolus (Miniature hybrids)
- Sunny position
- Good well-drained garden soil
- Plant 10-15cm (4-6in) deep

These plants grow to 45-90cm (18-36in) tall, and the flower spikes are about 35cm (14in) long, with each flower about 5cm (2in) across. They bloom after midsummer, and flowers are often frilled or fluted. The colours are bright, and varied with blotches, spots and stripes.

These corms are best grown in a sunny part of the garden in a good well-drained soil; they should be planted 10-15cm (4-6in) deep, depending on the soil – plant deeper in light soil to give better anchorage. In heavy soil, add plenty of sharp sand under and around the corm to aid drainage, keep the young plant weeded, and water well once the flower spike starts to open. Lift the plant in autumn, remove the young corm and store it in a frost-free place for the following year. Keep the plant free from disease with a fungicide; if the plant wilts and turns yellow, destroy it to stop the virus disease spreading to others.

Take care
Do not grow in waterlogged soil. 76♦

Gladiolus (Butterfly hybrids)
- Full sunshine
- Good garden soil
- Plant 10-15cm (4-6in) deep

This plant is noted for the unusual markings on the throat of the blooms. They are 60-120cm (24-48in) tall, with flower spikes 45cm (18in) long; the alternating blooms, 10cm (4in) across, appear in summer. Flowers range from white through yellow, orange, or red to purple, with blotches, markings or edgings in contrasting colours.

They thrive in a sunny place in good well-drained soil. In light soils, plant corms 15cm (6in) deep, but in heavier soils this can be reduced to 10cm (4in). Plant out in spring, and start watering in early summer. The plant should be lifted in autumn when its leaves turn yellow. Leave it to dry for a few days, and the new corm will come away from the old one easily; store it through the winter in a frost-free place for the next year. Treat these plants with a fungicide.

Take care
Protect from frost.

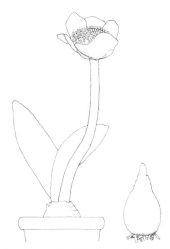

Gloriosa rothschildiana

(Glory lily)
- **Light shade**
- **Balanced potting mixture**
- **Plant just under the surface**

These tender plants should be treated as greenhouse or pot plants unless you live in a very mild area. They have a climbing and trailing habit, and may reach 180cm (6ft) tall. The leaves are glossy, with a tendril at the leaf end which hooks onto supports. The striking flowers, 10cm (4in) across, have curved back petals of scarlet edged with golden yellow, and it blooms constantly through summer and autumn.

Plant the tuber in early spring in the greenhouse, at a temperature over 16°C (60°F). Use a 17.5cm (7in) pot. Water freely while it is growing, and give a liquid manure once a week until flowering has finished. The tuber should be kept dry through the winter in a cool but frost-free place. During summer provide a support, and shade it from direct sun. Seeds take up to four years to flower. Offsets taken in early spring and grown in pots will flower in two years.

Take care
If leaves fall early, allow the plant to almost dry before watering again.

Haemanthus natalensis coccineus

(Blood lily)
- **Sun or partial shade**
- **Balanced potting mixture**
- **Just cover with soil**

This tender greenhouse bulbous plant has long thick leaves that hug the ground and develop after the flowers have died. It forms a 5-7.5cm (2-3in) head of red blooms in late summer. The large bulb is 7.5cm (3in) in diameter, from which grows a plant only 20-30cm (8-12in) tall.

Plant the bulbs in a pot in spring. Leave them undisturbed for several years, but give them a liquid feed every two weeks throughout the summer. When the leaves dry off, put the pot in a cold place until growth starts again, early the following spring, when the soil should be moistened. Every few years take the bulb out and use fresh soil for repotting; offsets can be removed and potted up as separate bulbs, and should flower in two years' time. A 20cm (8in) pot of John Innes No. 2 potting mixture is ideal. Mealy bugs may attack the plant, leaving tufts of waxy wool; paint the areas with a systemic insecticide.

Take care
Do not disturb the root.

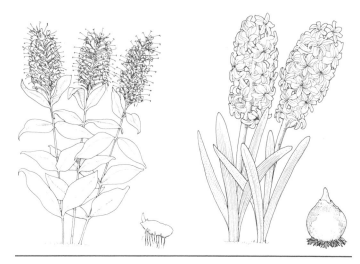

Hedychium gardnerianum
(Ginger-wort)
- Sun or light shade
- Rich potting mixture
- Plant just below the surface

This tender plant will grow outdoors only in very mild areas, and is usually grown as a pot plant. It is a perennial, 180cm (6ft) tall and 150cm (5ft) across; the leaves are often 30cm (12in) long and as broad. In summer it has spikes of scented yellow flowers 5cm (2in) wide, with brilliant scarlet stamens.

Due to its size, this plant needs a tub. Use John Innes No. 3 potting mixture supplemented with a liquid feed every two weeks during the growing period. In autumn the stems should be cut down almost to the rhizome. Let the plant rest in winter, keeping it dry. In early spring water it a little, increasing the amount as it grows. The plant can be repotted in spring when it starts to shoot; at this stage divide and replant the rhizomes to increase your stock. If grown outdoors, plant it in a sheltered place in summer and lift before the first frost.

Take care
Do not water during the winter.

Hyacinthus orientalis
(Dutch hyacinth)
- Full light but not direct sun
- Bulb fibre
- Plant with tops showing through the surface

This plant consists of a cluster of strap-like leaves around a central flower stem that bears a spike of scented bell-shaped blooms. The plant will reach 23cm (9in) tall and the flowerhead may be 15cm (6in) long. If potted in late summer the prepared bulb will bloom in winter; autumn planting gives spring bloom. The flowers may be white, yellow, pink, red, blue, purple or mauve, and some have double blooms.

Plant bulbs in a mixture of peat with shell and charcoal – this mix is known as bulb fibre. The fibre should be moist at all times, but keep the shoots dry – if they become wet they rot and die. Keep in a cool dark place for at least eight weeks to encourage root growth, then bring out into warmth and full light (but not direct sunlight) once the flower shoot has fully emerged from the bulb. Dutch hyacinths are usually trouble-free.

Take care
Keep bulb fibre moist, not wet. 78♦

Hyacinthus orientalis
(Garden hyacinth)
- Full sun or light shade
- Ordinary garden soil
- Plant 12.5-15cm (5-6in) deep

These hyacinths flower in spring with bright scented blooms on a stem over 30cm (12in) long, and 15cm (6in) of the stem is covered in flowers. They are ideal bedding plants either in formal arrangements with other plants or in clumps to give patches of colour. They can be propagated from seed but may take six years to reach the flowering stage; it is far better to obtain specially prepared bulbs produced by professional bulb growers. These are planted in ordinary garden soil in autumn; choose a site in full sun or light shade. After flowering they can be lifted and moved to another part of the garden to recuperate, leaving space for other plants to provide summer colour. Treat the soil with a general pesticide to keep pests away. If disease occurs, with poor leaf and flower production, destroy the bulb to prevent spreading.

Take care
Buy bulbs from a good specialist. 78♦

Hymenocallis × festalis
- Full sun, sheltered from frost
- Rich well-drained soil
- Plant with top just level with surface

This plant is susceptible to frost; unless your garden has a near frost-free climate, treat it as a pot plant. The white scented flowers, 10cm (4in) across, have a centre not unlike a daffodil trumpet, but the outer petals are long and slender. The strap-like leaves are 30cm (12in) long. The plant grows to 45cm (18in) tall, and blooms in spring if grown as a pot plant; out of doors it flowers in summer.

When growing this as a pot plant use a medium or large pot with a general potting mixture. For early blooms keep it at 16°C (60°F), but for later flowers keep the greenhouse just frost-free. In spring give a mild liquid feed every two weeks. Keep it in shade, and water well in hot weather; repot every two or three years. For outdoors grow it in a pot and plant out in late spring in a well-drained soil in full sun. Generally this plant is trouble-free.

Take care
Protect from frost. 79♦

Ipheion uniflorum
- Full sun
- Ordinary soil with good drainage
- Plant 5cm (2in) deep

Iris (Pogoniris/Arillate)
(Bearded irises)
- Sunny position
- Rich light soil with some lime
- Plant 2.5-7.5cm (1-3in) below surface of soil

These bulbous plants are noted for their grass-like sea-green leaves and star-shaped flowers. The plants grow only 20cm (8in) tall, with spring flowers 5cm (2in) wide; the white to deep lavender-blue blooms are scented.

Bulbs should be planted in autumn. Plants should be kept weeded, and when leaves and flower stems die back in summer they should be removed. Position plants in full sun in well-drained soil. The bulbs are increased by bulblets, the plants should be lifted in autumn, divided, and replanted at once. Do this every two or three years to keep the plants free-flowering and healthy. Make sure bulbs do not dry out or become wet during transplanting, and keep the time out of the soil to the minimum. Ipheions are generally trouble-free provided the soil is kept free-draining.

Irises of the Pogoniris group have fleshy, hairy beards on the three outer petals (the *falls*). The three inner petals are called the *standards*, and between these are three strap-like petals known as the *style arms*. Within the Pogoniris section there are two groups: the first of these, the Arillate group, has a branching rhizome root that grows 2.5-7.5cm (1-3in) below the soil surface. Sword-like leaves sprout from the rhizome in a fan-like growth, and 12.5cm (5in) flowers are borne in early summer on a single stem up to 60cm (24in) tall. Colours are mainly white, blue and brown, with veining and markings. Rhizomes should be protected from excessive wetness. When foliage dies the plants may be lifted and divided. Use a pesticide and fungicide.

Take care
Do not let bulbs dry out or get wet when planting or transplanting. 78-9►

Take care
Do not let soil become too wet.

Iris (Pogoniris/Eupogon)

(Bearded irises)
- **Full sun**
- **Ordinary garden soil**
- **Plant with the top of the rhizome exposed**

Irises of this group are distinguished by the rhizomes that lie on the surface, by the scented flowers and by the blue-green sword-like leaves. Size varies from 7.5cm (3in) to 150cm (5ft) according to the variety; the dwarf members will thrive in rock gardens, and the taller varieties are suitable for the herbaceous border. Blooms appear from early to late spring in a wide range of colours and sizes. Many of the flowers are heavily veined, and up to 15cm (6in) across. These are delightful plants that help to fill the gap between spring and summer flowering plants.

Give them a sunny place with ordinary garden soil. Rhizomes should be planted either at midsummer or in early autumn. Keep them moist until established. Plants can be divided to increase stock. Use a pesticide and fungicide to keep plants healthy.

Take care
Cut leaves back in winter to stop slug attack. 80♦

Iris (Apogon/ Californicae)

(Beardless irises)
- **Sun or partial shade**
- **Acid or neutral garden soil**
- **Plant 2.5cm (1in) deep**

The leaves of these plants are slender, sword-shaped and normally evergreen. The flowers are up to 9cm (3.6in) across in late spring. Colours range from white through cream, yellow, orange and pale blue to deep purple; some have heavy marking on the falls and the three outer petals.

These irises are short-lived, but are easily grown from seed. This can be harvested from the plant and sown in autumn, in a temperature of about 10°C (50°F). Plant seedlings out when they are still very young to avoid later root disturbance; they should flower the following year. Rhizomes can be divided in autumn and replanted, but keep the roots moist until they are established. Poor-quality specimens should be thrown out to keep the rest healthy. Treat with a pesticide and fungicide, and destroy diseased plants.

Take care
Keep freshly planted rhizomes and young plants moist. 97♦

Iris (Apogon/Hexagona)
(Beardless irises)
- **Sun or light shade**
- **Moist rich soil**
- **Plant just below the surface**

This group has large six-ribbed seed pods, up to 10cm (4in) long. The leaves are narrow and evergreen. The flowers, up to 20cm (8in) wide, appear in midsummer; the zig-zag stems carry a flower bud and leaf at each change of direction.

   The plants reach a height of 90cm (36in) and should be planted 40cm (16in) apart in a moist soil, with the rhizome just below the surface. Choose a site in either sun or light shade, and a rich soil that has a high humus content. In winter protect the plants with a layer of straw, compost or leaf-mould. There are a number of hybrids: of the named varieties, 'Wheelhorse' and 'Dixie Deb' have grown exceptionally well in temperate areas. Protect the plants with a general insecticide and fungicide; if plants become badly affected they should be lifted and destroyed to stop the trouble spreading.

Take care
Keep the rhizomes moist.

Iris (Apogon/Laevigatae)
(Beardless irises)
- **Full sun**
- **Grow in moist soil and water**
- **Just below surface of soil, or 7.5-15cm (3-6in) under water**

These irises thrive on the banks of streams, rivers, ponds and lakes. *I. laevigata, L. pseudacorus* and *I. versicolor* are water irises for the garden pool, but *I. kaempferi* should be planted in moist soil but not directly into water. The blooms of the kaempferi irises are particularly beautiful in both colouring and form. The flowers may grow up to 20cm (8in) across, in either single or double form. All these irises have the characteristic sword-shaped leaves, and all will grow up to 60cm (24in) tall except *I. pseudacorus,* which reaches 120cm (4ft) in water.

   Plant rhizomes just under the soil, or between 7.5-15cm (3-6in) under water. Lift the plants every three years, and divide and replant. Treat the plant with a general pesticide and fungicide to keep trouble to a minimum. Take particular care to prevent chemicals entering the water.

Take care
Do not let plant or rhizome dry. 99♦

Iris
(Apogon/Sibirica)
(Beardless irises)
- Sunny position
- Moist garden soil
- Plant 2.5cm (1in) deep

These irises grow well both in the border and by water. They are noted for their grass-like leaves, their hardiness and their summer flowers. Plants can reach 90cm (36in) tall, but most grow to only 60cm (24in). The flowers come in various colours and shadings and can measure 10cm (4in) across.

Hybrids are readily available from nurseries in autumn. Plant them in moist soil, but if next to water the rhizome must be at least 15cm (6in) above the water level to prevent rot. If the soil is dry, give it a good watering, and add humus to conserve moisture. Plant rhizomes 2.5cm (1in) deep in a sunny situation and avoid hoeing around the plant as the root system is very near the surface. Mulch well in spring to deter weed growth. The plants can be lifted in late autumn or early spring and divided and replanted; do this every four years or so.

Take care
Do not hoe around the root area.

Iris
(Apogon/Spuria)
(Beardless irises)
- Sunny situation
- Ordinary garden soil
- Plant 5cm (2in) deep

These hardy irises have fibrous rhizomes, and double ridges on the seed pods. The leaves are sword-shaped, in some varieties growing to 90cm (36in) long; the leaves die down in winter leaving young fresh growth to last through to spring. The white, purple, yellow or deep blue flowers are up to 10cm (4in) wide, and some are scented.

Plant the rhizomes 5cm (2in) deep in good garden soil that has plenty of sun; water them well in and keep the surrounding soil moist. Once planted, in late autumn, they should be left alone; only dig them up if the flowers become small because they are too crowded. This should be done in late autumn; divide the root and replant with more space. It will take up to two years for them to start flowering again. Treat these irises with a pesticide and fungicide.

Take care
Do not disturb the plant unnecessarily.

Iris (Crested section)

(Crested irises)
- **Partial shade**
- **Moist lime-free soil with humus**
- **Plant just below the surface**

These irises have orchid-like flowers with a cock's-comb crest instead of a beard. The smaller varieties are suitable for the rock garden as they grow only 15cm (6in) tall, with flowers over 5cm (2in) across; larger ones reach 45cm (18in) high, with flowers 7.5cm (3in) wide. The leaves are evergreen, broad, and glossy. The delicate blooms are white or lavender, with markings and spots.

The thin rhizomes should be planted in late spring, just under the surface; the soil should have a plentiful supply of humus – leaf-mould or peat – mixed with it. This should be topped up every spring with a mulch of extra humus. These irises can be lifted after flowering, divided and replanted with extra space around the rhizomes, but keep them moist until they are established. Shelter them from the sun in frosty weather so that they can thaw out gently. Protect them from slug and snail attacks with bait.

Take care
Keep moist in dry weather. 98♦

Iris (Juno/I. bucharica var.)

(Bulbous irises)
- **Sheltered site**
- **Light well-drained soil**
- **Plant 5cm (2in) deep**

These irises come from Turkestan and will grow to a height of 45cm (18in). Attached to the bulb are thick fleshy delicate roots, and if these are damaged the plant suffers. The leaves do not last long. Scented yellow and cream flowers appear in spring, over 5cm (2in) wide and up to seven blooms on each stem.

If you have an exposed site, grow these bulbs in pots and keep them protected until the weather is mild enough to plant them outside. Plant the bulbs in early autumn in a light well-drained soil that will keep dry in summer; if possible, position them among shrubs or under trees to provide shelter. After the leaves have died down, the plant can be lifted. Allow the roots to become limp and less fragile, tease out the bulbs, divide them and replant with more space around them. The plants should be treated with a pesticide and fungicide.

Take care
Avoid damaging the roots. 98♦

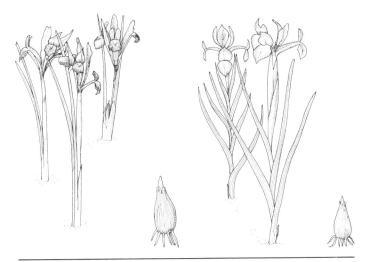

Iris (Reticulata/I. reticulata var.)

(Bulbous irises)
- **Light shade or sun**
- **Light well-drained limy soil**
- **Plant 5-7.5cm (2-3in) deep**

These hardy Asian bulbous plants have a net of fibres around the outside of the bulb and grass-like tubular leaves that are dark green with a paler tip. They are early flowering; some start at midwinter and others follow successively through to spring. The flowers are often 7.5cm (3in) wide, in lemon-yellow and blue. These plants are small, and ideal for the rock garden; they rarely grow more than 15cm (6in) tall.

Plant them in a light well-drained chalky soil; if the ground is heavy, the bulb may not shoot after the first year. Give each bulb a covering of 5-7.5cm (2-3in) of soil. They do best when planted in autumn. After flowering give a liquid feed every four weeks until the bulb dies back. If grown for indoor decoration, plant them in pots, keep in the cool until the flower buds show, then bring into the warm. Use a fungicide and pesticide to keep the plants healthy.

Take care
Do not plant in heavy moist soil. 101♦

Iris (Xiphium/I. xiphium var.)

(Bulbous irises)
- **Sunny site**
- **Good well-drained garden soil**
- **Plant 10-15cm (4-6in) deep**

In less temperate areas this iris is tender and short lived, but hybrids (known as Dutch, Spanish and English irises) are more vigorous and hardy. The English iris prefers a moist rich soil and should be left undisturbed; it flowers in summer with a range of colour that does not include yellow, the blooms reaching 12.5cm (5in) across, and it will grow to 60cm (24in) tall. The Dutch iris flowers from early summer and prefers a light soil, the 10cm (4in) wide blooms come in a wide range of colours, and grow to a height of 60cm (24in). The Spanish iris follows the Dutch flowering period, and is smaller, but the flowers have fine smoky shades; they enjoy a lighter, drier and warmer soil than the others.

Lift and ripen the bulbs by drying them in late summer and then replant in autumn where the soil is heavy. In warm light soils they can be left in the ground. Protect the plants with a pesticide and fungicide.

Take care
Soak in fungicide before planting.

Ixia viridiflora hybrids
(African corn lily)
- **Sunny situation**
- **Sandy soil**
- **Plant 7.5cm (3in) deep**

Ixiolirion pallasii
(Ixia lily)
- **Sheltered sunny position**
- **Well-drained soil**
- **Plant 7.5cm (3in) deep**

These plants are noted for their six-petalled star-shaped flowers in a variety of yellows, reds, purples or blues, up to 5cm (2in) wide. These flowers are borne on strong wiry stems up to 45cm (18in) tall, so they are good for cutting.

Ixias are not hardy, but will grow out of doors in milder parts of the temperate zone; otherwise they can be grown as pot plants. The corms should be planted during autumn in a sunny situation, in ordinary or sandy soil. To protect corms from frost, a good layer of ashes, bracken or compost should be spread over the area in late autumn before the frosts start. For pot growing, plant in the autumn and water in, then keep dry until the corms sprout; keep a temperature just above freezing but under 7°C (45°F). The plant can be lifted after flowering, and the offsets removed and replanted in autumn; seeds take up to three years to flower.

This elegant bulbous plant grows to 40cm (16in) tall, with long slender grey-green leaves. From spring to early summer it has fine displays of tubular flowers of a deep lavender blue, almost 5cm (2in) wide; these are popular for use as cut flowers.

The small bulbs should be planted in autumn, 7.5cm (3in) deep and 15cm (6in) apart, in a spot that is sheltered but sunny, in well-drained soil that has had plenty of leaf-mould added. For a good show of blooms these plants require a period of hot dry weather. The bulbs do best when they are left undisturbed; if they multiply and become overcrowded, the offsets can be removed in autumn when the leaves and flowers have died down, and planted in a nursery bed until they are mature enough to be planted out in their final flowering positions. To keep the plants healthy use a pesticide and fungicide.

Take care
Protect from frost.

Take care
The soil must not be too moist.

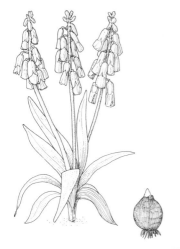

Lachenalia aloides/tricolor

(Cape cowslips)
- **Maximum light**
- **Rich potting mixture**
- **Plant 2.5cm (1in) deep**

These are generally grown as indoor pot plants, although they can be used for hanging baskets, but as their flowering period is from midwinter to spring they are better for the conservatory rather than out of doors. They have pale strap-like leaves, sometimes spotted or marked with lavender, and will grow up to 30cm (12in) in height. The 2.5cm (1in) bell-shaped flowers are usually yellow in colour but often marked with orange or green.

The bulbs should be planted in a rich soil, six bulbs to a 15cm (6in) pot. Soak the soil after planting, leave it dry until the bulbs start to sprout, then water moderately until fully grown. Give a liquid feed then once a fortnight until the leaves turn yellow, allow the bulbs to dry off, and repot them into fresh soil in late summer. At this time small bulblets can be removed and grown separately in pots, and will reach flowering size in about two years.

Take care
Do not store bulbs over winter. 100♦

Leucojum aestivum 'Gravetye Giant'

(Snowflake)
- **Light shade**
- **Moist soil**
- **Plant 7.5cm (3in) deep**

These snowdrop-like plants have sword-like leaves. The large drooping bell flowers are produced in spring, 2.5cm (1in) long, in white with the petals tipped with green. 'Gravetye Giant' is an improved form, growing 50cm (20in) tall.

These plants prefer a moist soil, in which they should be planted 7.5cm (3in) deep and positioned so that they can enjoy some shade. They should be planted in late summer or early autumn, and left undisturbed for several years until they become too crowded, with too few blooms. Then, when the leaves have turned yellow they can be lifted, divided and replanted immediately, 20cm (8in) apart. This is a better way to increase your stock than by growing from seed, which can take six years to reach flowering size. These leucojums do not like drying off in summer so it is important to keep them moist. They are normally both pest- and disease-free.

Take care
Keep plants moist in droughts. 100♦

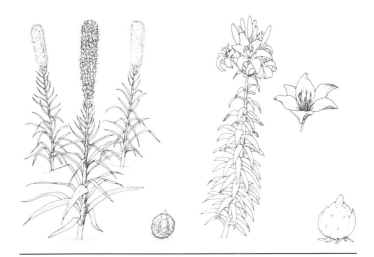

Liatris spicata

- Open sunny site
- Heavy wet soil
- Plant 5cm (2in) deep

This hardy tuberous plant grows to 90cm (36in) tall. It has a lily-like stem, which ends in a dense spike, 15-38cm (6-15in) long, of pinky purple flowers in early autumn.

These plants enjoy an open sunny place with plenty of moisture in the soil, even tolerating boggy sites. The tubers should be planted in early autumn or early spring, up to 45cm (18in) apart and 5cm (2in) deep, if the soil is moist; where soil is drier, plant deeper and add plenty of humus to retain moisture. A heavy mulch of compost or well-rotted manure will keep moisture from evaporating too quickly, and extra water should be given during dry periods. Remove dead flowers; and as the plant loses all its leaves, the spot must be marked to prevent damage through digging or hoeing during the winter. In spring the plant can be lifted, divided and replanted every few years to increase your stock; grown from seed it will take two years to flower.

Take care
Keep moist during droughts.

Lilium Asiatic cultivars (Division 1)

- Full sun or semi-shade
- Well-drained garden soil
- Plant 10-15cm (4-6in) deep

These are early-flowering lilies with blooms growing either singly or in groups springing from the same point on the stem. These cultivars grow up to 150cm (5ft) tall, with some flowers reaching 15cm (6in) across. Some forms have hanging flowers with petals curled back to form a 'Turk's cap'. Blooms appear at midsummer with a variety of colours, shapes and markings.

The bulbs should be planted 10-15cm (4-6in) deep in well-drained garden soil, in full sun or semi-shade, during the winter months. During the growing season they should be kept moist with plenty of water and mulching with peat, compost or leaf-mould. Every few years the plants can be lifted in the winter months, divided and replanted with more space around them. Seed will take up to three years to reach flowering. The plants should be treated with a general pesticide and fungicide.

Take care
Keep plants moist during the growing period. 102♦

Lilium Martagon hybrids (Division 2)

- Partial shade or light woodland
- Well-drained garden soil
- Plant 10-15cm (4-6in) deep

These hybrid lilies flower from late spring onwards. They are easily grown, and reach 150cm (5ft) tall, with flowers up to 7.5cm (3in) wide in white, cream, yellow, orange or deep red, with spots and markings on the petals.

They thrive in partial shade, tolerate lime, and require a good well-drained soil with plenty of leaf-mould, compost and well-rotted manure mixed into it to retain moisture in dry periods. The bulbs should be planted 10-15cm (4-6in) deep in the winter months, and left undisturbed for several years. During winter they can be lifted, divided and replanted with more space around them to increase stock; seeds take three years to mature to flowering size. Treat plants with a general pesticide and fungicide, and spread some slug bait on the soil.

Take care
Divide in rotation, as they take a year to recover.

Lilium candidum cultivars (Division 3)

- Full sun
- Ordinary well-drained soil
- Plant 10cm (4in) deep

These lilies grow to 180cm (6ft) tall, and in summer they have flowers 7.5cm (3in) long, with very curved petals. These blooms are scented, in yellow, orange and white with bright red pollen. The original parent, *L. candidum*, has been cultivated for over 3,500 years and revered by many civilizations.

Bulbs should be planted 10cm (4in) deep in autumn in a well-drained garden soil containing plenty of humus. To obtain a succession of flowers over the years, a few plants each year should be lifted, divided and replanted, as they take at least a year to recover. Seeds take up to three years to reach flowering size, so it is quicker to increase your stock by division. If weather conditions are bad for planting, put the bulbs in damp peat until the soil is ready, to stop them drying out. Lilies are attacked by a variety of ills; use a pesticide, a fungicide and slug bait.

Take care
Keep bulbs moist when transplanting, and be sure to stake mature plants.

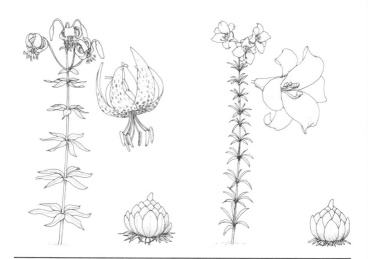

Lilium American cultivars (Division 4)

- Light shade
- Well-drained acid soil
- Plant 15cm (6in) deep

These varieties, grown from crossing American lilies, produce a range of plants that can reach 210cm (7ft), with 7.5cm (3in) blooms in yellow, orange and reds, some in two-colour forms with markings and spots.

   Plant bulbs 15cm (6in) deep in a well-drained neutral to acid soil with plenty of peat, leaf-mould or compost. These cultivars give best results if grown in light shade. The bulbs should be left undisturbed, with a mulch of leaf-mould and bracken each winter. They can be lifted in late autumn, divided and replanted to give the bulbs more room, but treat only a few each year, as they take a season to recover. Give the plants a general pesticide and fungicide to keep them free from trouble. Use a slug bait to stop slug or snail damage to young shoots, but use the bait under a tile to prevent other animals reaching it.

Take care
Stake plants to prevent wind damage. 103♦

Lilium longiflorum cultivars (Division 5)

- Full sun
- Limy soil
- Plant 10cm (4in) deep

These plants are crosses of lilies from Japan and Taiwan and are generally half-hardy and generally recommended as pot plants, although the variety 'Holland's Glory' is highly regarded for outdoor cultivation as well, with its large white strongly scented blooms. It grows to a height of 120cm (4ft).

   The bulbs should be planted at a depth of 10cm (4in), in soil fortified with leaf-mould or compost to hold moisture during drought periods. They should be left undisturbed for several years; then they should be lifted in the autumn, divided and replanted with more space around each bulb. An autumn mulch of leaf-mould or compost is very beneficial, but do not use fresh manure because this will rot the roots. These lilies are prone to disease and care should be taken to treat them with a fungicide. If disease appears after treatment, lift the affected plant and destroy it. A pesticide will keep attacks from pests to a minimum.

Take care
Watch for disease.

Above: **Iris innominata (Apogon/Californicae)**
A beautiful beardless iris with evergreen leaves that thrives in a fibrous soil. It likes both sun and light shade and blooms in late spring. 87▸

Left: **Iris bucharica**
A Juno iris that is a bulbous plant and has scented yellow or white blooms in spring. It needs to be sheltered and kept on the dry side in summer. It can be grown as a pot plant but be sure to use a deep pot. 90♦

Right: **Iris kaempferi (Apogon/Laevigatae)**
A beardless iris that enjoys a moist soil. Developed in Japan to give a wide range of colours and forms, it flowers in early summer. 88♦

Below: **Iris gracilipes**
This small crested iris bears flowers in spring and is very suitable for planting in rock gardens provided it is sheltered and partially shaded. Ideally the soil should be acid and kept on the moist side. 90♦

Left: **Lachenalia aloides 'Van Tubergen'**
This is suitable as a pot plant, giving a good show of blooms through the winter provided the temperature does not drop too low. In summer it can be used in hanging baskets. 93▸

Right: **Leucojum aestivum 'Gravetye Giant'**
A late spring-flowering plant that likes a moist soil with some shade. Placed in a shrubbery or light woodland it will thrive and need little attention for several years. 93▸

Below: **Iris reticulata 'Jeanine'**
A bulbous iris that is very popular for the rock garden and border. It blooms in late winter and early spring and prefers a light chalky soil. Also suitable for growing indoors. 91▸

101

Above:
Lilium 'Cover Girl' (Division 1)
An Asiatic lily with large wide open blooms that provide colour in a border in sun or semi-shade. 94♦

Below:
Lilium 'Enchantment' (Division 1)
A vigorous Asiatic lily with up to 16 outstanding cup-shaped flowers to a stem. Enjoys a sunny position. 94♦

Above:
Lilium 'Shuksan' (Division 4)
The petals on this American lily curl right back to form a 'Turk's cap'. The plant will grow as tall as a person and is ideal for the back of the border. 96♦

103

Above left:
Lilium 'Life' (Division 6)
A tall-growing Aurelian lily that makes a beautiful feature in a lightly shaded garden border. 113♦

Above: **Lilium 'Imperial Crimson' (Division 7)**
A scented Oriental lily with large blooms in the summer months. 113♦

Left: **Lilium regale**
A hardy and popular lily that enjoys full sun and ordinary soil. Scented flowers in midsummer. 114♦

Right: **Lilium tigrinum splendens**
Well known for its spotted petals and 'Turk's cap' form. 114♦

Left: **Narcissus cyclamineus**
*An early spring-flowering dwarf
narcissus that makes an ideal rock
garden plant, where its unusual
backward-facing petals and grass-
like leaves can be appreciated.* 115♦

Right:
Narcissus pseudonarcissus
*A small narcissus that naturalizes
well in light woodland or in grass,
where its blooms can be enjoyed in
spring. Plant in moist soil.* 116♦

Below: **Muscari armeniacum**
*The grape hyacinth prefers full sun
and will thrive in rock gardens and
borders, forming clumps of brilliant
blue flowers in spring. It will thrive in
ordinary garden soil.* 115♦

Above: **Narcissus 'Fortune'**
(Division 2)
*A large-cupped narcissus that gives
a fine display in the spring. The bulbs
should be planted in a good moist
soil in light shade.* 117♦

Left: **Narcissus 'Rembrandt'**
(Division 1)
*A large trumpet narcissus that makes
an outstanding show in the spring
months. It can be forced for earlier
blooming indoors.* 117♦

Right: **Narcissus 'Ice Follies'**
(Division 2)
*Ideal for growing in the garden for
spring flowers, this large-cupped
narcissus needs light shade and
moist soil. Can be forced in pots.* 117♦

Above: **Narcissus
'Irene Copeland' (Division 4)**
*A double narcissus that makes an
effective contrast to the single form.
It is particularly attractive as a cut
flower in an arrangement.* 118♦

Below: **Narcissus
'Grand Soleil d'Or' (Division 8)**
*A bunch-flowering narcissus that
produces an abundance of blooms to
each bulb. An excellent pot plant for
indoor flowers in early spring.* 120♦

Above: **Narcissus 'Bartley'
(Division 6)**
This delightful small narcissus has N. cyclamineus *as a parent, which shows in its swept back petals. Ideal for the front of borders.* 119♦

Above: **Narcissus 'Actaea'**
(Division 9)
This well-known scented poeticus *narcissus has white petals and a* *small flat frilled cup. It usually flowers* *after the other groups.*121♦

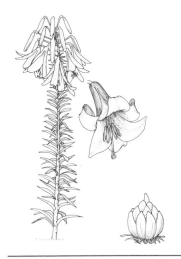
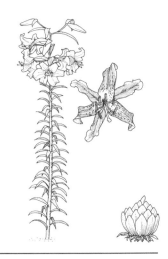

Lilium Trumpet and Aurelian cultivars

(Division 6)
- Partial shade
- Rich well-drained soil
- Plant 15cm (6in) deep

Grouped in this section are the funnel-shaped, bowl-shaped, pendent and star-like blooms that are mainly crosses from the Aurelian lilies. Some are lime-tolerant, but others are not. They grow to 210cm (7ft), and should be planted 30cm (12in) apart in a rich well-drained soil in partial shade at a depth of 15cm (6in). Most of this group are hardy, but a mulch of leaf-mould or compost spread over them in autumn will protect the less hardy from frost. The flowers, many of them scented, are often over 12.5cm (5in) across, and some reach 20cm (8in) wide. A wide range of colours is available; some have stripes, others are bicoloured or flushed with other shades. The flowering period is in late summer. The bulbs can be lifted in the winter months, divided and replanted, but make sure that they do not dry out. Use a pesticide and fungicide to keep the plants healthy.

Take care
Stake the taller lilies. 104♦

Lilium Oriental cultivars

(Division 7)
- Full sun
- Rich well-drained gritty soil
- Plant 15cm (6in) deep

These hybrid forms of Oriental lilies are often sub-divided into flower shapes: trumpet, bowl, star or flat and the very curved petal forms. The flowers appear in summer, and sometimes reach 25cm (10in) across; many are scented, and they have very decorative shapes in a wide range of colours, often marked, striped and spotted. The plants grow to a height of 210cm (7ft) and should be planted at a distance of 30cm (12in) apart and at a depth of 15cm (6in) in a rich, well-drained but gritty soil with plenty of humus.

Place them in full sun and as they grow stake them against being blown over. A mulch of humus in early spring is advisable. The bulbs can be lifted in the late autumn or winter months, divided and replanted with more space around them, but make sure that they do not lose moisture. Seeds take up to three years to flower.

Take care
Do not let the bulbs dry out when planting or replanting. 105♦

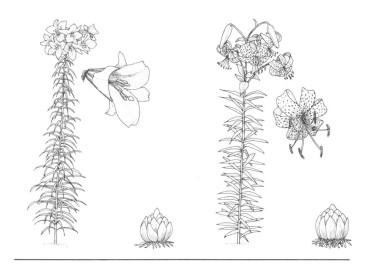

Lilium regale
(Regal lily)
- **Full sun**
- **Well-drained garden soil**
- **Plant just below the surface**

This lily originates from China, is very popular and is probably the best-known of all lilies, with its scented white funnel-shaped flowers up to 12.5cm (5in) long, blooming in summer. The centres of the flowers are brilliant yellow, and the backs of the petals have red-purple shading. These lilies can reach 180cm (6ft) but most grow to 120cm (4ft) tall.

Regal lilies require to be placed in full sun in a well-drained soil, with or without lime, and they will spread quickly. The bulbs should be planted just below the surface; some experts recommend planting as deep as 23cm (9in), but this is advisable only in a very light and free-draining soil. Bulbs can be lifted, divided and replanted during the winter months, without letting them dry out. Seeds take up to three years to reach maturity, and most people prefer to grow lilies from bulbs. In exposed areas they should be staked to prevent wind damage.

Take care
Keep the bulbs moist when planting or transplanting. 104♦

Lilium tigrinum
(Tiger lily)
- **Full sun**
- **Well-drained lime-free soil**
- **Plant 15cm (6in) deep**

This spectacular lily is a native of China, Korea and Japan and is grown for its very curved petals that give it a 'Turk's Cap' 10cm (4in) long in late summer. The bright orange or red-orange petals are spotted with black, and have dark red pollen on the anthers. There is a variety that has bright yellow blooms with purple spots, known as *L.trigrinum flaviflorum*. The plants can reach 180cm (6ft).

Bulbs should be planted at a depth of 15cm (6in) in a well-drained lime-free soil, 23cm (9in) apart. Grow this separate from other lilies, because it is prone to virus disease. Keep the soil moist throughout the growing season; it helps to add plenty of humus to the soil. Increase by picking off the *bulbils* – tiny bulbs that grow between the leaves and the stem at flowering time. They should come off easily. Plant them just under the soil surface in pots, keep for a year, then plant out. Watch for virus attack, and treat with pesticide.

Take care
Keep soil moist in droughts. 105♦

Muscari armeniacum
(Grape hyacinth)
- **Full sun**
- **Ordinary well-drained soil**
- **Plant 7.5cm (3in) deep**

The grape hyacinth has tight bell-like blue flowers grouped closely together like miniature inverted bunches of grapes on single stems in spring. The plants grow to a height of 25cm (10in), with an equal spread after the leaves separate at flowering time.

Plant the bulbs 7.5cm (3in) deep in a well-drained ordinary garden soil in full sun; shade will encourage leaf growth and less flowers. After a few years the bulbs will become congested and after the leaves turn yellow the plants need to be lifted, divided and replanted immediately. Sometimes the plants seed themselves; otherwise you can take the seed in summer, sow it in pans, and keep it cool in a cold frame. The seedlings can be transplanted the following year, and will come into flower in another year or so. The plants are normally pest-free, but occasionally the flowers are spoilt with smut, making black sooty areas; destroy plants to stop it spreading.

Take care
Plant in sun for good flowering. 106♦

Narcissus cyclamineus
- **Sun or partial shade**
- **Moist well-drained soil**
- **Plant 5cm (2in) deep**

Like all members of the narcissus and daffodil family, this species has the typical cup and petals, but the petals are turned back. The plant comes from Spain and Portugal, is small, only 20cm (8in) tall, and the trumpets are 5cm (2in) long. This dwarf habit makes it ideal for the rock garden, where its fine delicate form and dark green grass-like leaves keep it in scale with other low-growing plants. The yellow flowers bloom in early spring, and do equally well in the open or in partial shade provided the soil is moist.

Plant the bulbs 5cm (2in) deep and 5cm (2in) apart. They will seed themselves, or in late summer they can be lifted, divided and replanted to allow more space. Treat the plants with a pesticide and fungicide to keep troubles to a minimum, but if damage is bad it is better to destroy the plant.

Take care
Keep soil moist in dry periods. 106♦

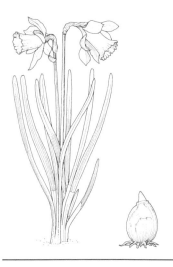
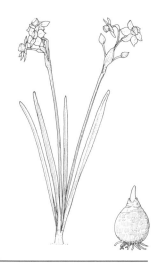

Narcissus pseudonarcissus

(Wild daffodil; Lent lily)
- **Sun or light shade**
- **Moist soil**
- **Plant 5cm (2in) deep**

This plant has strap-like leaves, and grows to a height of 30cm (12in). The flowers have bright lemon trumpets with very pale yellow petals 5cm (2in) across, and appear in spring. They thrive in a good moist soil, among low grass or in open woodland. They are good for naturalizing where a small daffodil will be in scale.

This species is easy to grow in a moist soil, and will be happy in either sun or light shade, where it should be planted at a depth of 5cm (2in). If the soil and the situation are to its liking, it will thrive and spread vigorously, forming clumps. After a few years it is advisable to lift the bulbs after the leaves have died back, divide them and replant with 7.5cm (3in) between bulbs. A more natural look is obtained by casting the bulbs over the area and planting them where they have fallen. Use a pesticide and fungicide to keep plants healthy.

Take care
Keep the plants moist, especially in hot weather. 107♦

Narcissus tazetta

(Bunch-flowered narcissus)
- **Sun or semi-shade**
- **Moist soil**
- **Plant 7.5-10cm (3-4in) deep**

This group of narcissi comes from a wide area spreading from the Canary Islands, through the Mediterranean, North India to China and Japan and is characterized by the bunch of blooms on the flower stem of a single flower. The leaves are strap-like, and the plant will grow to a height of between 30 and 45cm (12-18in). The blooms have white petals 3.8cm (1.5in) wide, with a shallow yellow cup. They have a strong perfume, and will flower in winter – among the earliest to bloom. They are often grown in pots, as some of the varieties are half-hardy.

The bulbs should be planted 7.5-10cm (3-4in) deep in a well-drained moist soil where there is either full sun or partial shade. Gently cast the bulbs over the ground and plant them where they fall, to give a natural random spacing. Every few years the clumps of plants should be lifted, divided and replanted with more space around them to grow.

Take care
Avoid waterlogged soil.

Narcissus Division 1
- Light shade
- Moist well-drained soil
- Plant 7.5-10cm (3-4in) deep

Narcissus Division 2
- Light shade
- Well-drained moist soil
- Plant 7.5-10cm (3-4in) deep

In this group the plants all have only one flower to a stem, and the trumpet or cup is longer than the petals. It has been further sub-divided into sections with trumpet and petals yellow, trumpet yellow and petals white, trumpet and petals white, and any other combination. These are all of garden origin, and will grow to 45cm (18in) tall. In this group are most of the popular daffodils, such as 'King Alfred' and 'Golden Harvest', with large blooms and fluted trumpets 7.5cm (3in) wide in spring.

These do equally well in the garden or forced in pots for earlier flowering. They should be planted in a good moist soil in late summer. Where they are grown in grass, do not use a mower until the leaves have turned yellow and the goodness of the soil has been taken up by the bulbs. Lift and divide the bulbs every few years to encourage large blooms and extra stock. Use a pesticide and fungicide.

Take care
Do not cut leaves until yellow. 108♦

These are large-cupped narcissi with one flower to each stem, and the cup or trumpet is more than one third the length of the petals but no longer than them. The group has been sub-divided into sections with the cup darker than the petal colour; cup coloured and petals white, and cup and petals white. The cups may be frilled, serrated or plain, and the colours are white, yellow, orange pink or red. Among the highly prized varieties are 'Fortune', 'Carlton', 'Desdemona', 'Royal Orange', 'Ice Follies' and 'Tudor Minstrel', which has blooms of over 12.5cm (5in) across. Most of these grow to a height of 45cm (18in).

The mid-green strap-like leaves should be left to turn yellow and die back without tying them into knots, as this is the period when the bulb takes up nutrition for the next season. Increase by division in the autumn every few years. Use a pesticide and fungicide.

Take care
Keep moist in droughts. 108-9♦

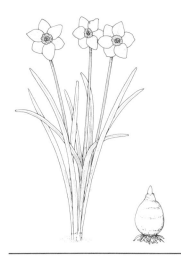

Narcissus Division 3
- Semi-shade
- Rich well-drained moist soil
- Plant 7.5-10cm (3-4in) deep

This group is of garden origin and
has small cups with only one flower
to each stem, and the cup is less than
one third of the length of the petals –
smaller than in Division 2. It has been
sub-divided into sections with petals
and cup coloured, petals white and
cup coloured, and all white. Of these,
'Birma' has yellow petals and
orange-scarlet cup; 'Enniskillen' has
white petals and crimson-red cup;
and 'Angel' has white petals and
white cup, and is 12.5cms (5in) wide.
These bloom in early spring and
grow to a height of 45cm (18in),
giving a splendid show in the garden
especially where grown in clumps
and drifts.

Plant in light shade in late summer,
as soon as the bulbs become
available. Leave them undisturbed
for a few years before lifting and
dividing to allow more space around
them; this will encourage large
blooms, provided the leaves have
not been knotted or cut when they
finish flowering. Use a pesticide and
fungicide to keep down attacks.

Take care
Keep bulbs moist in droughts.

Narcissus Division 4
- Light shade
- Rich well-drained soil
- Plant 7.5-10cm (3-4in) deep

This group all have double flowers,
one or more to each stem, and they
grow 38-50cm (15-20in) tall. Some
are scented, and others have
dramatic flower forms: the well-
known 'Irene Copeland', 'White
Lion', and 'Golden Ducat' are all
included in this section.

Bulbs should be planted in late
summer, as soon as they become
available in the shops, in a rich well-
drained soil with 7.5-10cm (3-4in) of
soil over them, and in semi-shade.
Leave them for a few years before
lifting and dividing the bulbs to
increase your stock. This should be
done after the leaves have turned
yellow and died; they should not be
touched before this as the plant uses
this period to store food for the
coming season. Grow them in
clumps and drifts; for the best effect,
cast the bulbs over the ground and
plant them where they fall, which will
give an informal spacing. The plants
should be treated with a pesticide
and fungicide to keep them healthy.

Take care
Keep moist during dry periods in
spring and summer. 110♦

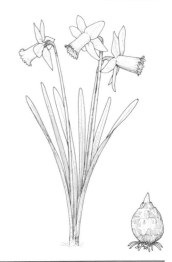

Narcissus Division 5

- Partial shade
- Good well-drained soil
- Plant 5cm (2in) deep

Some of the most delicate and graceful small narcissi are included in this group. Most have back-swept petals on their spring blooms. They are divided into two sub-sections: those that have the cup more than two-thirds of the length of the petals, and those that are less than this measurement. Within this group are *N. triandus albus* ('Angel's Tears'), with white flowers; and 'Tresamble', also white, with as many as six blooms to a stem. These are small plants, many less than 30cm (12in) tall but they make up in beauty what they lack in stature.

The bulbs should be planted 5cm (2in) deep in a well-drained but good garden soil, with partial shade to keep the soil moist in late spring and summer, when the plant stores up goodness for the following spring. After a few years the bulbs can be lifted in late summer, divided and replanted. They look well sited in rockeries and alpine gardens. Use a pesticide and fungicide to guard the plant against attack.

Take care
Keep the plants moist in droughts.

Narcissus Division 6

- Light shade
- Good well-drained soil
- Plant 5-7.5 (2-3in) deep

These cyclamineus narcissi are noted for their long trumpets and swept-back petals. The group is divided into those with the trumpet more, and those with it less, than two-thirds of the petal length. Of these plants there are some lovely small specimens that are ideal for the garden and for forcing to use indoors during the winter. In the garden their small stature, 20-38cm (8-15in), makes them suitable for rock gardens and the front of borders. The varieties 'February Gold', 'Peeping Tom' and 'Beryl' are representative of this section.

The bulbs should be planted in late summer when they become available, with 5-7.5cm (2-3in) of soil over them in a lightly shaded area with a good well-drained soil that has been enriched with leaf-mould and compost to improve its moisture-holding properties during drought periods. Lift and divide the bulbs every few years to increase stock. Treat plants with pesticide and fungicide to protect them.

Take care
Plant bulbs soon after purchase. 111▶

Narcissus Division 7

- Partial shade
- Enriched garden soil
- Plant 5-7.5cm (2-3in) deep

These are the jonquil narcissi, noted for their perfume, tubular leaves and yellow flowers up to 5cm (2in) across. Here again the division is grouped into those with large and small cups, with two-thirds of the petal length being the critical measurement. Most in this division will grow about 30cm (12in) tall, and some of the lovely single and double forms appear early: 'Waterperry' flowers in midwinter, and the beautiful 'Jonquilla Double' about a month later. These have dainty flowers and should be placed where their beauty can be seen properly, in containers, raised beds and on banks.

The bulbs should be planted 5-7.5cm (2-3in) deep in late summer, in an enriched garden soil with a high humus content but free-draining. After flowering the leaves should be left untouched; only when they die right back should they be removed. Every few years the plants can be lifted, divided and replanted to give space for development.

Take care
Avoid waterlogged soil.

Narcissus Division 8

- Light shade
- Well-drained moist soil
- Plant 7.5-10cm (3-4in) deep

These are descended from *N. tazetta* and have the same characteristic of bunch flowering. The majority of the hybrids are on the tender side, and should be grown for pot cultivation rather than for outdoors. Those that do thrive out of doors vary considerably, some blooming at midwinter, but others not till late spring. Generally they grow to about 40cm (16in) high, with sword-like leaves; the highly scented blooms are in a variety of colours, single and double. The best-known are 'Geranium', 'Winston Churchill', 'White Cheerfulness' and 'Yellow Cheerfulness'.

The bulbs enjoy a well-drained soil with plenty of humus, and a lightly shaded position, with 7.5-10cm (3-4in) of soil over them. Plant bulbs in late summer, as soon as you can obtain them; this is also the time for lifting, dividing and replanting. Use a pesticide and fungicide to keep the plants healthy.

Take care
Do not cut or remove the leaves until they die right down. 110♦

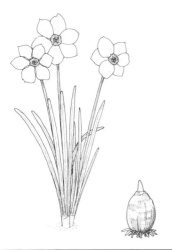

Narcissus Division 9
- Semi-shade
- Well-drained rich soil
- Plant 7.5-10 (3-4in) deep

These are the poeticus narcissi and are characterized by the white petals and the flat frilled bright red cup of the scented flowers; they usually appear after the other narcissi have finished blooming. The plants grow about 38cm (15in) tall, and the flowers reach 7.5cm (3in) across. The varieties best known are 'Actaea', 'Constable' and 'Old Pheasant Eye'.

Plant the bulbs in late summer as soon as they are available in the shops, 7.5-10cm (3-4in) deep, in rich well-drained soil that has plenty of humus added; the site needs to be lightly shaded. The leaves should be left untouched until they die right back, so that they can take up food for the coming season. When the bulbs become conjested, they should be lifted in late summer, divided and replanted with more space around them. Keep small bulbs in a nursery area until large enough to plant out. Keep pest and disease attack to a minimum with a pesticide and fungicide.

Take care
Keep moist during droughts. 112♦

Narcissus Division 10
- Partial shade
- Good garden soil
- Plant 2.5-5cm (1-2in) deep

In this section the Royal Horticultural Society has placed all the wild forms and wild hybrids, and all the miniature and less spectacular narcissi. These are ideal for rockeries, alpine gardens, containers and for naturalizing in the wilder parts of the garden. Some of these have curious forms and tiny blooms: among the noteworthy are *N. bulbocodium conspicuus* (Yellow hoop petticoat), 15cm (6in) high; *N. minimus,* the smallest of all trumpet daffodils, only 7.5cm (3in) tall; and *N. minor pumilis plenus*, a 15cm (6in) daffodil with double blooms.

The smaller bulbs need to be planted in late summer, with only 2.5cm (1in) of soil over them, but the larger bulbs can have double this amount. Position them in partial shade, in a good free-draining garden soil with plenty of humus. Spread the bulbs in a natural drift or series of clumps to give an informal look. They can be lifted in late summer, divided and replanted to increase stock.

Take care
Avoid waterlogged soil.

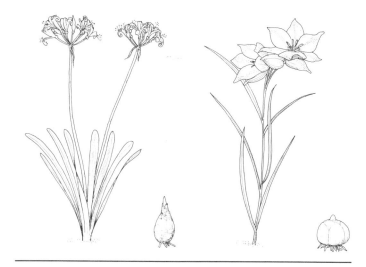

Nerine bowdenii

(Guernsey lily)
- **Sunny position**
- **Ordinary well-drained soil**
- **Plant just under the surface**

Nerine bowdenii, which comes from South Africa, is sufficiently hardy to withstand most winters in the temperate zone. It will grow to a height of 60cm (24in). The blooms open in autumn, with up to eight flowers in each cluster; the clusters are 15cm (6in) across, usually rose or deep pink, but there is also a white form. The mid-green leaves are narrow and strap-like.

The bulbs should be planted in either late summer or early spring, and in an ordinary well-drained soil and in a sunny position. The bulbs are placed just under the surface or, if the soil is light, they can be set deeper – as much as 10cm (4in). Where there are bulbs near the surface they should be covered with a thick layer of bracken, leaf-mould or compost to protect them against frost. They can be lifted in spring, divided and replanted to encourage larger blooms. Watch for mealy bugs and treat them with pesticide.

Take care
Keep moist when growing. 129♦

Nomocharis saluenensis varieties

- **Light shade**
- **Deep moist soil**
- **Plant 7.5-10 (3-4in) deep**

Nomocharis, a member of the lily family, grows to a height of 120cm (4ft). It has narrow leaves, and the saucer-shaped flowers are often 10cm (4in) across in summer; they are carried on a stem that will bear five or six white or pink blooms tinged with purple.

Plant them in early spring, in a soil that is deep and moist, and in the light shade. The bulbs should have 7.5cm (3in) of soil over them, but if the soil is light this can be increased to 10cm (4in). Cover the area each spring with a layer of compost, leaf-mould or peat. The bulbs are easily damaged: take care when planting, and avoid transplanting or digging around the roots. Increase your stock by taking seeds and sowing them in autumn or spring; grow in pots for a year, and plant out the following spring. Nomocharis plants are usually disease-free, but treat the surrounding soil with slug bait to deter slugs and snails.

Take care
Avoid damaging the roots.

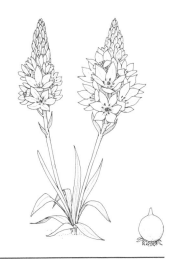

Notholirion thomsonianum

- **Full sun**
- **Moist well-drained soil**
- **Plant 7.5cm (3in) deep**

This bulbous plant has its origins in the Western Himalayas, where it grows among rocks and in areas of stunted trees and shrubs. It can reach 80cm (32in) tall. It has highly perfumed blooms of white or rose, 5cm (2in) long, on flower stems not unlike a widely spaced hyacinth spur, in spring, with up to 20 bell-shaped flowers on the stem.

Plant the bulbs 7.5cm (3in) deep in full sun, if possible with some protection (such as a wall or fence) to keep off cold winds, in a well-drained soil that has had plenty of leaf-mould, peat or compost added to increase its moisture-retaining properties. The bulbs flower well if the plant is kept dry in summer, and this will encourage the bulb to ripen for the following season. Every few years, lift and remove offsets and grow them on separately in a nursery bed. Notholirions can also be grown as a pot plant in a cool greenhouse.

Take care
Keep the plants dry in summer.

Ornithogalum thyrsoides

(Chincherinchee)
- **Partial shade**
- **Good soil or potting mixture**
- **Plant 10cm (4in) deep**

This plant from South Africa has up to 30 white, cream or yellow star-like flowers grouped in a tight cluster at the top of the 45cm (18in) stem in summer. The mid-green leaves spring from the base of the plant and grow 30cm (12in) long. It is not hardy in the temperate zones where frosts occur, and should be grown in a pot.

Plant the bulbs in a 20cm (8in) pot of rich potting mixture in autumn and keep in a cool greenhouse for early spring flowering. In mild areas the bulbs can be planted out of doors in spring, with 10cm (4in) of soil over them; they should be well covered during the winter months with a thick mulch of bracken, leaf-mould or peat. Seeds can be sown but they will take up to four years to reach flowering size. Generally these are pest-free, but if sooty spots appear on the leaves, treat them with a fungicide, and if this has no effect, destroy the plant to stop the fungus spreading to other plants.

Take care
Protect against frost. 130♦

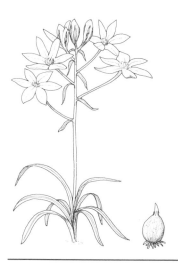
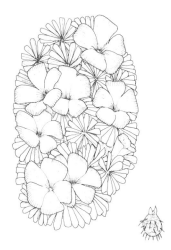

Ornithogalum umbellatum

(Star of Bethlehem)
- Partial shade
- Ordinary well-drained soil
- Plant 7.5cm (3in) deep

This plant grows to a height of 30cm (12in), with a spread of up to 20cm (8in). In spring, the flower stem carries a profusion of white star-like blooms with green stripes on the outside. The plant is hardy, and ideal for edgings and mass effects, even naturalizing in short grass or in shrubberies.

Plant the bulbs in autumn, in ordinary well-drained soil with 7.5cm (3in) of soil over them in an area where there is some shade; if possible, dig in a good quantity of peat, compost or leaf-mould beforehand. Once planted they need no attention and will continue to produce masses of blossom. To increase stock, lift the clumps of bulbs in late summer after the leaves have died down, divide them, and replant with more space. Seeds can be sown, but take up to four years to reach flowering size. Most ornithogalums are pest-free, but watch for fungus attack on leaves.

Take care
Keep plants moist in droughts.

Oxalis adenophylla

- Full sun
- Sandy peaty soil
- Plant 5cm (2in) deep

These 7.5cm (3in) tall bulbous plants are ideal for the rock garden and edges of borders. They have delicate cup-shaped lilac-pink flowers 2.5cm (1in) wide in midsummer, and small clusters of leaves that die down in winter.

The bulb-like rhizome should be planted in spring or autumn in a soil that is sandy but enriched with peat, leaf-mould or compost. Plant it 5cm (2in) deep in a sunny place, although it will stand partial shade. When the bulbs have finished flowering in summer, they can be lifted, divided and replanted with more space around them. This can also be grown as a decorative pot plant, using a 20-25cm (8-10in) pot and ordinary potting mixture such as John Innes No. 1. Keep it in the cool until ready to flower, and then bring it indoors. Every alternate year move it to a larger pot with fresh soil, or divide it and keep in the same size pot with new potting mixture.

Take care
Keep the plant moist during drought.

Pancratium maritimum

(Sea lily)
- **Sunny protected site**
- **Well-drained soil**
- **Plant 20cm (8in) deep**

These half-hardy bulbous plants grow out of doors only where there is shelter from frost; otherwise it is necessary to keep them in a frost-free greenhouse. The plant has narrow grey-green strap-like leaves and heavily scented white flowers in summer; they have an inner cup and six narrow petals with green stripes on the outside, and are 7.5cm (3in) wide. The plant grows 30cm (12in) tall and has a similar spread.

Place the bulbs 20cm (8in) deep in a well-drained soil, in a place sheltered from cold winds. They should be planted as soon as they become available in the autumn, and kept just moist during the winter. As the leaves grow increase the water until flowering finishes. In autumn the plant can be lifted, and offsets removed and grown on in pots until they are large enough to flower. Replant the parent bulbs and cover them with a thick layer of bracken, peat or leaf-mould.

Take care
Protect from frost.

Polianthes tuberosa 'The Pearl'

- **Full sun**
- **Well-drained soil or potting mixture**
- **Plant 2.5cm (1in) deep**

This tuberous-rooted plant is tender and should be grown as a pot plant unless your garden is frost-free. The mid-green leaves are strap-like and grow from ground level. The white flowers, like tubular stars, are arranged in terminal spikes up to 120cm (4ft) long. The blooms are among the most scented available and 'The Pearl' is a double variety flowering in late summer.

In autumn plant the bulb 2.5cm (1in) deep in a well-drained soil or a good potting mixture. In a 12.5cm (5in) pot, it can be kept in the greenhouse during winter, and brought indoors to bloom in late summer. Keep a series of plants at different stages by controlling the temperature, to produce flowers throughout the season. Keep in as light a place as possible to encourage sturdy growth, with just a little water until it is grown; then water freely. Purchase fresh tubers each year; offsets rarely flower.

Take care
Keep in a frost-free place.

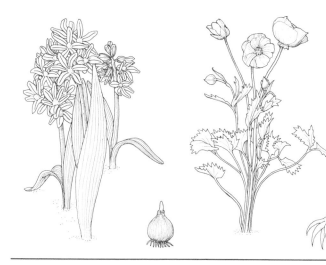

Puschkinia scilloides

(Striped quill)
- **Sun or partial shade**
- **Good sandy garden soil**
- **Plant 5cm (2in) deep**

This spring-flowering bulbous plant from Asia Minor is highly suitable for growing in low grass, in rockeries, or as a pot plant in a cool greenhouse. It grows to a height of 20cm (8in), with mid-green strap-like leaves and six-petalled bell-shaped flowers of silvery-blue, 1.25cm (0.5in) long, with a greenish blue stripe in the centre of each petal. There are up to six blooms on each stem.

In autumn, plant the bulbs 5cm (2in) deep in a good sandy garden soil, in either sun or partial shade, and leave them untouched unless you need to increase your stock. This can be done when the leaves have died down; lift the plants and remove offsets, dry them and then replant. This is far quicker than growing by seed, which can take up to four years to mature. Where possible leave the plants to form mats or carpets of flowers in drifts under mature trees or shrubs. The only pests that cause trouble are slugs, so lay slug bait.

Take care
Do not disturb the roots. 130♦

Ranunculus asiaticus

- **Sunny position**
- **Ordinary garden soil**
- **Plant 5cm (2in) deep**

These plants are hardy in milder areas, but in colder parts they should be kept in a frost-free place during winter. Most of these plants have deeply cut leaves of mid-green, and semi-double blooms up to 7.5cm (3in) wide that are fine as cut flowers because they last well.

At first sight they look a little like anemones, with flowers of crimson, pink, orange, gold or white.

They bloom in early summer, and should be placed in the sun in a good soil that has been well dug over with plenty of compost, peat or well-rotted manure added. The tubers should be planted at any time from midwinter to spring, 5cm (2in) deep, with the claw-like roots pointing downwards. In less mild areas the plant should be lifted when its leaves turn yellow; dry off the root system in the sun, and store in a frost-free place until replanting in spring. At this time the tubers can be divided to increase your stock.

Take care
The claw-like roots must point downwards. 131♦

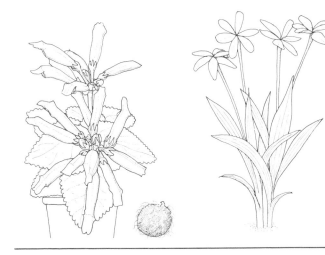

Rechsteineria cardinalis
- Shady site
- Good potting mixture
- Plant level with the surface

These tender plants from South Africa are grown as pot plants for their decorative foliage of green velvety leaves, and their scarlet tubular flowers, 5cm (2in) long. Usually they bloom in summer, but by staggering the sowing times the flowering season can be extended. They grow 23-45cm (9-18in) high.

The dormant tubers are started by putting them in moist peat at a temperature of 21°C (70°F). When the sprouts are almost 5cm (2in) long, put them into separate 15cm (6in) pots of John Innes No. 2, with the tops of the tubers level with the surface. Feed every two weeks with a liquid manure, and keep the temperature above 16°C (60°F). When they have finished flowering the leaves turn yellow. Leave off watering, remove dead growth and store for the winter in a frost-free place. In spring they should be potted up again. At this time the tubers can be divided so that each section has at least three shoots.

Take care
Do not bury tubers below surface.

Rhodohypoxis baurii
- Full sun
- Well-drained moist soil
- Plant just below the surface

These South African plants grow to only 7.5cm (3in) high, with a spread of 15cm (6in), and they have hairy pale sword-like leaves. The flowers have six petals, the three inner ones standing a fraction higher than the three outer ones; blooms vary from white to deep red, 3cm (1.25in) in diameter, and appear from spring to autumn.

Plant the corm-like rhizomes in autumn in a well-drained but moisture-retentive lime-free soil, with a good sunny position. In wet winters, put a cloche over the plants to keep them dry, and it will also give some protection against frost. Lift the plant in autumn to remove the offsets; replant these and they should flower the following year. Where excessive cold and damp occurs, treat them as pot plants. Grow them in 15cm (6in) pots of well-drained lime-free mixture, watering frequently until autumn; then repot, allow to almost dry and water as the plant begins shooting.

Take care
Avoid excessive wetness in winter.

Schizostylis coccinea
(Kaffir lily)
- **Sunny situation**
- **Moist soil**
- **Plant 2.5cm (1in) deep**

This elegant plant from South Africa grows to 90cm (36in). It has long slender leaves and spikes of up to ten star-shaped bright red or pink flowers almost 5cm (2in) across on each stem during autumn.

The rhizomes should be planted in spring in a moist place; they will even do well at the edge of water. Put them 2.5cm (1in) deep in a rich and fertile soil. A spring mulch of peat, compost or leaf-mould will help to keep the roots moist; if the soil dries out, water well. The growth remaining in late autumn should be cut down; cover the area with a layer of bracken to protect the roots against hard frost. As the plants are vigorous, they need lifting and dividing every few years, in spring. Make sure that each section of rhizome has several shoots, and plant them in their flowering positions. Treat with both a pesticide and a fungicide to keep them free from attack.

Take care
Keep the plants watered in summer and in droughts. 132◆

Scilla peruviana
(Cuban lily)
- **Warm sunny position**
- **Moist well-drained soil**
- **Plant 5cm (2in) deep**

This scilla is a bulbous plant from the Mediterranean with glossy strap-like leaves sometimes 30cm (12in) tall. The flowers vary from white through blue to dark purple, in late spring. The flowerheads have up to 100 star-shaped blooms, each about 2cm (0.8in) across.

The plants are easy to grow and need little after-care. They are recommended for rock and alpine gardens, growing in short grass or for indoor use in pots and containers. The bulbs should be planted 5cm (2in) deep in a moist but well-drained soil; add plenty of peat, leaf-mould or compost to improve the moisture-retention of the soil. The site should be warm and sunny. Put the bulbs out in late summer or early autumn, as soon as they become available. Scatter the bulbs over the area and plant them where they fall; this will give a casual and natural look. At this time offsets can be taken off mature plants and replanted to increase stock.

Take care
Keep moist during droughts.

Above: **Nerine bowdenii**
This fine showy plant bears lovely, deep pink flowers in the autumn. It enjoys a warm sunny border backed with a wall for protection against cold winds and frosts. 122♦

Above: **Ornithogalum thyrsoides**
This attractive, summer-flowering plant needs a sheltered position to grow well. If you live in a cold area treat it as a pot plant, it will then bloom in the early spring. 123♦

Right: **Ranunculus asiaticus**
An early summer-flowering plant that thrives in a sheltered sunny place and produces a succession of blooms that last well in water. The tubers increase in good soil. 126♦

Below: **Puschkinia scilloides**
This small plant produces its unusual blooms during the spring. It is ideal for rock gardens or as a pot plant and will tolerate full sun or partial shade. Leave it undisturbed. 126♦

Above:
Schizostylis coccinea 'Major'
A moisture-loving plant that flowers *in autumn with red or pink blooms.* *These are vigorous and need to be* *divided every few years.* 128♦

Above: **Scilla sibirica
'Atrocoerulea'**
*These vivid blue spring flowers are
best kept separate from other blue
plants, which may look dull.* 145♦

Below: **Scilla tubergeniana**
*A much paler scilla that blooms as
soon as it emerges from the soil in
late winter. This low-growing plant is
ideal for rock gardens.* 145♦

Left: **Sinningia 'Orchidosena'**
*The gloxinia produces brilliant
blooms from its tuber and makes a
fine outdoor container plant; if the
night temperatures are right it will
flower well. It can be used as an
indoor plant but avoid direct sun.* 146♦

Right: **Sprekelia formosissima**
*A most unusual flower is produced
by this half-hardy plant from Mexico.
It enjoys full sun or light shade and a
rich soil. It can be used for outdoor
show, but give it some protection
against cold winds and frost.* 147♦

Below: **Sternbergia lutea**
*An autumn-flowering plant that looks
like a crocus and gives a show of
brilliant yellow flowers. With its love
of sun and its small stature it makes
an ideal subject for the rockery.* 147♦

Above: **Tigridia pavonia 'Rubra'**
*A succession of vivid and unusual
blooms adorns this plant in summer.
The strange markings and spots
amply justify its common name of
tiger flower. Grow in full sun.* 148♦

Left: **Tecophilaea cyanocrocus**
*A low-growing rockery plant that
thrives in a sandy soil in a sheltered
place. Avoid too much wetness,
especially in the winter, and protect
against frost. Blooms in spring.* 148♦

Right: **Tritonia crocata**
*These delicate flowers appear in late
spring in a wide range of colours.
Use this plant as a container subject
or as an indoor pot plant; in either
situation it enjoys full sunshine.* 150♦

Above: **Tulip 'Ida' (Division 4)**
*A Triumph tulip that blooms in mid-season and thrives in full sun.
Provide some lime in the soil.* 152♦

Left: **Tulip 'Hadley' (Division 1)**
*The large-flowered, single early
bloom comes in the spring and
makes a good formal plant.* 150♦

Right: **Tulip 'Trance' (Division 3)**
*A Mendel tulip that blooms in mid-spring. It prefers a sunny site where
there is some lime in the soil.* 151♦

Far right:
Tulip 'Montgomery' (Division 3)
*These Mendel tulips, with striking
margins, would grace any garden.* 151♦

Above: **Tulip
'Golden Apeldoorn' (Division 5)**
*A superb tall-growing and large-
flowered Darwin hybrid.* 152♦

Above right:
Tulip 'Aladdin' (Division 7)
*A Lily-flowered tulip with typical
waisted bloom and pointed petals.* 153♦

Right:
Tulip 'Greenland' (Division 8)
*The open bloom of this Cottage tulip
appears in mid-season.* 154♦

Below:
Tulip 'Orajezon' (Division 6)
*These popular bedding Darwin tulips
bloom in late spring.* 153♦

Above: **Tulip 'Gold Medal'
(Division 11)**
*Enormous, double late blooms are
characteristic of this group.* 155♦

Left: **Tulip 'Flaming Parrot'
(Division 10)**
*These large, exotic Parrot flowers
are heavily fringed.* 155♦

Below left: **Tulip 'Allegretto'
(Division 11)**
*Flamboyant, double late flowers that
are long lasting during the spring.* 155♦

Below: **Tulip 'Giuseppe Verdi'
(Division 12)**
*These small Kaufmanniana blooms
open out in sun like water-lilies.* 156♦

Above: **Tulipa tarda**
A small plant that is ideal in a rock garden. The flowers open wide in sunshine and can have up to six blooms on each stem. 157♦

Below: **Tulip 'Yellow Empress' (Division 13)**
A Fosteriana variety with open long-lasting flowers of a medium size in mid-spring. Enjoys the sun. 156♦

Scilla sibirica 'Atrocoerulea'
- Sun or partial shade
- Moist well-drained soil
- Plant 5cm (2in) deep

The leaves of these scillas appear in early spring followed by the flower stems, of which there are three or four to each bulb; each stem bears up to five brilliant deep blue bell-shaped flowers, almost 2.5cm (1in) long, in spring. Plant these separate from other blue flowers, as the vivid blue of the scillas makes other blues look dull. The form 'Atrocoerulea' (also known as 'Spring Beauty') is a great improvement on the common form, with larger flowers and a more vigorous habit.

They will grow in any well-drained soil that holds moisture in drought periods. The bulbs should be planted in late summer or early autumn at a depth of 5cm (2in) in an area of sun or partial shade where they can be left undisturbed. Remove offsets from mature plants in autumn, and replant. Scatter the bulbs over the ground and plant where they fall to give a natural look. Use a pesticide and fungicide to keep plants healthy.

Take care
Plant as soon as the bulbs become available. 133♦

Scilla tubergeniana
- Sun or semi-shade
- Moist well-drained soil
- Plant 5cm (2in) deep

This scilla comes from the mountainous meadows and rocks of North-west Iran and grows to a height of 10cm (4in), with a similar spread. The flowers are pale blue or white, and open as soon as they emerge from the soil.

The bulbs should be planted as soon as they are purchased, in late summer or early autumn, in a sunny or half-shaded area of the garden where the soil is moist but well-drained. Cover the bulbs with 5cm (2in) of soil. For a casual effect the bulbs can be cast gently over the area and planted where they fall. To increase the moisture-holding properties of the soil dig in a good supply of leaf-mould, peat or compost before planting. Once planted the bulbs can be left untouched, but to increase stock, offsets can be taken from mature plants after the leaves have died down, and placed in a nursery bed to grow. Seed may take five years to reach flowering size.

Take care
Keep moist in dry weather. 133♦

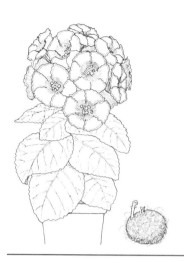

Sinningia speciosa
(Gloxinia)
- **Shade**
- **Fine peaty soil**
- **Plant with top level with soil**

Gloxinias, widely grown as pot plants, have the ability to flower from seed in five months provided the night temperatures are kept above 18°C (65°F). The leaves are velvety, fleshy and dark. The flowers are bell-shaped, with lobes around the open end, and up to 10cm (4in) long, in white, red, violet or purple, some with white edges. Both single and double forms are available. The plants grow to 25cm (10in) tall, with a spread of 30cm (12in).

Place tubers in moist peat in late winter, at a temperature of 21°C (70°F). As soon as the young shoots reach 5cm (2in), pot them in a peat-based mixture with the tuber top level with the surface; a 15cm (6in) pot to each tuber is adequate. Keep in a shaded greenhouse at above 18°C (65°F), and give a liquid feed every week while it is flowering. Cut down watering when the leaves turn yellow, and store until late winter. Gloxinias are generally trouble-free.

Take care
Keep the plants warm and moist. 134♦

Sparaxis tricolor
(Harlequin flower)
- **Warm sunny site**
- **Rich well-drained soil**
- **Plant 10cm (4in) deep**

This half-hardy plant is best grown as a pot plant unless you are in an area that is frost-free. It is noted for its flat blossoms, 5cm (2in) across, that appear in early summer. There are a number of flowers to each stem, in yellow, red, purple and white, sometimes with a number of colours on one bloom.

Plant corms in a well-drained but rich soil to a depth of 10cm (4in) in early winter, in a border that receives plenty of sun. The leaves will die down in summer, and the plant can be lifted, dried off and stored until early winter, when it can be planted again. When growing it in pots, put up to six corms in one 15cm (6in) pot, with a good potting mixture such as John Innes No. 2. Soak the pot well and then keep it dry until the leaves start to sprout; then water it until the leaves turn yellow, when it should be left to dry. Offsets can be taken at this time from a mature plant, and repotted immediately; they should flower in one year.

Take care
Protect against frost.

Sprekelia formosissima

- Full light or light shade
- Rich potting mixture
- Plant with neck just above soil

This Mexican half-hardy plant is grown as a pot plant for its funnel-shaped deep-red flowers. It grows 45cm (18in) tall with sparse strap-like leaves that appear after flowering has finished. The flower stems appear in spring, each stem bearing only one flower, 10cm (4in) wide.

Plant bulbs singly in 10cm (4in) pots of rich potting mixture such as John Innes No. 3 in late summer, with the neck of the bulb just above the surface. Keep the temperature over 8°C (45°F). Do not water until spring, then water with a liquid feed every two weeks from flowering until the leaves die back in summer. Repot in early autumn every few years, and at this time remove offsets and plant them in separate pots; they take up to four years to reach flowering. Look out for white tufts of waxy wool at the base of the leaves, caused by the mealy bug: use a systemic pesticide, painted on with a brush, to clear the attack.

Take care
Keep dry in autumn. 135♦

Sternbergia lutea

- Full sun
- Well-drained soil
- Plant 10-15cm (4-6in) deep

This plant from the Eastern Mediterranean and Iran looks like a crocus but flowers in autumn, with bright blooms up to 5cm (2in) long on a true stem. The strap-like leaves appear with the flower but remain small and immature until the following spring. The plant will reach a height of 15cm (6in), with a similar spread.

Plant the bulbs in late summer, 10-15cm (4-6in) deep in a well-drained soil, in a sunny part of the garden. Leave undisturbed until they become overcrowded, when they can be lifted in late summer, divided and replanted immediately to prevent drying out. The offsets can be removed and grown separately, and will mature and come into flower in one year. This plant can be grown with, or as an alternative to, autumn-flowering crocuses and will provide a show of brilliant yellow. Watch for mice eating bulbs; and if slugs attack the young growth, use a slug bait. Normally this plant is disease-free.

Take care
Leave undisturbed if possible. 134-5♦

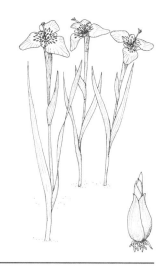

Tecophilaea cyanocrocus
(Chilean crocus)
- **Warm sunny place**
- **Rich sandy soil**
- **Plant 5cm (2in) deep**

This plant has a few slender twisted leaves growing to a height of 12.5cm (5in). Its deep blue to purple petals have white throats. In their natural habitat in Chile these plants grow on stony well-drained slopes.

Plant them out of doors in a rich sandy soil that drains well, in a sunny and warm position with some protection from hard frost. In wet areas cover with a cloche to keep the plant dry during the winter months; this will stop the growth of the leaves, which are susceptible to low temperatures, and the plant will pick up in the spring. Plant the corms 5cm (2in) deep in mid-autumn. They can also be grown as pot plants in a cool greenhouse: place six corms in a 15cm (6in) pot of moist potting mixture, leave without water until the leaves shoot, then water until the leaves die. Allow the plants to dry out in the greenhouse, remove any offsets and grow on separately to flowering size.

Take care
Protect from frost damage. 136♦

Tigridia pavonia
(Tiger flower)
- **Sunny location**
- **Rich well-drained soil**
- **Plant 7.5-10cm (3-4in) deep**

These spectacular half-hardy plants from Mexico and Peru can reach 60cm (24in) tall, with long sword-shaped pleated leaves of mid-green. The flowers last only a day, but each stem produces a succession of up to eight blooms in summer. These are up to 10cm (4in) wide, and have three large petals with three small petals in between, surrounding a cup-shaped base; the larger petals are plain but the smaller ones are spotted in white, yellow or red, which gives them the common name of tiger flower.

Plant the corms in spring, 7.5-10cm (3-4in) deep in a rich well-drained soil, in a position where there is plenty of sun. Lift them in autumn and keep dry and frost-free until replanting time next spring. At this time cormlets can be removed and grown separately, to reach flowering size in a couple of years. During winter guard against mice eating the stored corms.

Take care
Keep moist in dry weather. 136-7♦

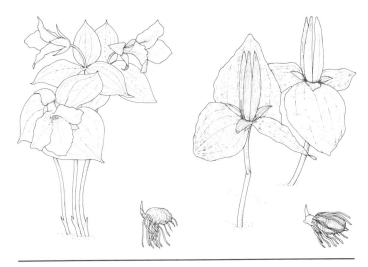

Trillium grandiflorum
- Shady situation
- Moist well-drained soil
- Plant 10cm (4in) deep

Trillium sessile
- Shady location
- Moist well-drained soil
- Plant 10cm (4in) deep

The trillium can grow to a height of 45cm (18in). It has pale to mid-green leaves, and large flowers 7.5cm (3in) across with the petals slightly turned back, blooming from mid-spring. The blooms are white on opening, gradually changing to pink; double varieties are available in white and pink.

Trilliums need a moist well-drained soil in a shady situation; added peat, leaf-mould or compost is beneficial. Rhizomes should be planted in late summer, as soon as they become available, at a depth of 10cm (4in). Planting in groups, with the bulbs 15cm (6in) apart, gives a massed effect. When leaves die down in late summer the plant can be lifted, and the rhizomes divided and replanted. Seeds can take up to six years to reach flowering size, so it is better to grow from rhizome sections, but make sure that each piece has a growing shoot on it.

Take care
Keep plants out of direct sun unless plenty of moisture is available.

This plant from central USA has deep green leaves marbled in grey, borne in a single group at the top of each stem. The stemless flowers have narrow, upright and partially twisted pointed petals that are often 7.5cm (3in) long; they are highly perfumed, and red to deep red in colour, blooming from mid-spring.

They thrive in a moist soil that is well-drained, with some leaf-mould, peat or compost mixed in to increase its moisture-holding qualities in hot weather. The plants can survive in direct sun if they have sufficient moisture, but most prefer cooler shady areas. The leaves die back in late summer, and at this time they can be lifted, divided and replanted, but each section of rhizome must have a growing shoot. Seeds are very slow to germinate, and can take up to six years to flower. Prevent slug attack with slug bait spread around the plants. Trilliums are usually disease-free.

Take care
Keep these plants moist.

Tritonia crocata
- Full light
- Good potting mixture
- Plant 5cm (2in) deep

This plant has fans of slender, sword-shaped mid-green leaves, and will grow to a height of 45cm (18in). In late spring it will produce a number of cup-shaped flowers up to 5cm (2in) wide, in white, yellow, pink, orange or copper.

Most of this group of plants are best grown as pot plants, although some can be used in late spring as container plants in the garden. Corms should be planted in moist potting mixture such as John Innes No. 2, five to a 15cm (6in) pot. After planting in early autumn, the pot should not be watered until the leaves start to shoot, unless the mixture dries right out. Keep a temperature of over 7°C (45°F) and put the plant in full light as much as possible. After flowering keep well watered until the leaves die back, then let the soil dry out in the greenhouse heat until early autumn, when it should be repotted. At this time offsets can be removed from the larger corms and grown on.

Take care
Support leggy plants with canes. 137▶

Tulip Division 1: Single Early
- Full sun
- Slightly alkaline soil
- Plant 15cm (6in) deep at most

Tulips were introduced into Europe from Turkey over 300 years ago and an industry for developing bulbs and hybrids has centred in Holland. In these pages, tulips have been split up into the official groups.

The single early is self-descriptive, single blooms in spring when grown out of doors, or in winter if forced under glass. The flowers grow to 12.5cm (5in) wide, and sometimes open flat in direct sunshine. A wide range of colours is available, in white, yellow, pink, red, orange, purple and mixtures. The plants, 15-38cm (6-15in) tall, are ideal for bedding or border planting.

Plant in late autumn in a slightly alkaline soil, in full sunlight, 15cm (6in) deep. When the petals fall, cut off the head to allow leaves and stem to feed the bulb for the following season. Offsets can be removed in late autumn and grown on. Use a pesticide and fungicide.

Take care
Dead-head the plants to build up the bulbs for next year. 138▶

Tulip Division 2: Double Early

- **Full sun**
- **Alkaline soil**
- **Plant 15cm (6in) deep at most**

This group of tulips has early-blooming flowers in spring, and if forced under glass can be in flower in late winter. The form is double, with blooms often reaching 10cm (4in) across. The plants grow to 30-38cm (12-15in), and leaves are often grey-green. A good example is 'Orange Nassau', a large blood-red tulip ideal for bedding out or forcing. The colours available are white, yellow, pink, orange, red, violet and purple, with many multicolours.

Plant out bulbs in late autumn in a slightly alkaline soil, 15cm (6in) deep. Tulips thrive in direct sunlight. When the petals fall, dead-head the plant but leave the stem and leaves to feed the bulb for the coming season. When the leaves turn yellow the plant can be lifted and stored for replanting in late autumn. Offsets can be taken at lifting time and grown on. Treat the plant with pesticide and fungicide.

Take care
Keep bulbs moist while growing.

Tulip Division 3: Mendel

- **Full sun**
- **Ordinary soil that is not acid**
- **Plant 15cm (6in) deep at most**

These tulips flower later than Divisions 1 and 2 and the blooms are more rounded, some 12.5cm (5in) across, and borne on slender stems. They flower in mid-spring, and colours include white, yellow, red and deep red. Representative of this division is 'Athleet', a lovely white tulip. Plants grow to a height of 50cm (20in), and the mid-green or blue-green leaves are shaped like a broad spear-head.

They enjoy an alkaline soil in full sun. Plant bulbs in late autumn at a depth of 15cm (6in), and water in well if the soil is dry. Keep moist during the growing period. When the petals fall, cut off the flowerhead to stop goodness concentrating on seed production to the detriment of the bulb. Bulbs can be lifted when the leaves turn yellow; remove offsets and grow on separately. The parent bulb can be dried and stored for replanting in late autumn. Treat the plants with a pesticide and fungicide to keep attacks to a minimum.

Take care
Keep moist while growing. 139♦

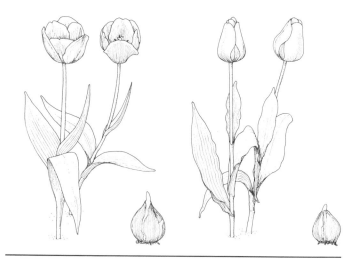

Tulip Division 4: Triumph

- **Sunny position**
- **Slightly alkaline soil**
- **Plant 15cm (6in) deep at most**

These tulips grow to 50cm (20in), and flower in mid-season, after the early singles and doubles but at the same time as the Mendel tulips in mid-spring. The blooms have an angular look and are carried on sturdy stems. The colours include white, yellow, orange, gold, pink, red and lilac. An example of this group is 'Garden Party', a white flower edged with pink.

These tulips thrive in a slightly alkaline soil in full sun. Bulbs should be planted at a depth of 15cm (6in) in late autumn; in light soils increase the depth to provide anchorage. Water in the bulbs and keep them moist during the growing period. After flowering cut the heads off to keep the nutrients feeding the bulb. When leaves turn yellow the plant can be lifted; remove offsets and grow on separately. Store the parent bulb in a dry place to ripen, before replanting in late autumn. Use a pesticide and fungicide to prevent attacks.

Take care
Keep dead-heading plants. 138-9♦

Tulip Division 5: Darwin Hybrids

- **Full sun**
- **Slightly alkaline soil**
- **Plant 15cm (6in) deep at most**

The tulips in this group are among the most brilliant and large-flowered. The leaves are grey-green and the plant grows over 60cm (24in) tall. Blooms reach 17.5cm (7in) wide when they open in mid-spring. The colours include yellow, orange, red and purple, with some spectacular multicoloured flowers. 'Golden Oxford' (a pure yellow), 'Big Chief' (one of the larger tulips grown, 65cm (26in) tall, with rose-coloured flowers) and 'Beauty of Apeldoorn' (a creamy yellow flushed with orange, with black base and anthers) are tulips that fall into this section.

These plants enjoy a slightly alkaline soil in full sun, and bulbs should be planted 15cm (6in) deep in late autumn. If the soil is dry, water well in and keep moist during the growing period. When the flowers have finished, cut off the heads to allow the stem and leaves to feed the bulb. Lift when the leaves turn yellow, remove offsets and plant separately.

Take care
In acid soils add lime or chalk. 140♦

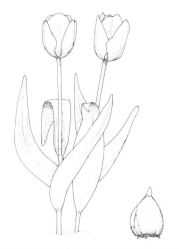

Tulip Division 6: Darwin

- Full sun
- Good soil that is not acid
- Plant 15cm (6in) deep at most

Within this group are the most popular bedding tulips, growing 75cm (30in) tall, with mid-green to blue-green leaves. The flowers are rounded and often reach 12.5cm (5in) across, blooming in late spring after the hybrids. Colours include white, yellow, orange, pink, red and purple, with a number of dramatic multicoloured varieties. Among many named tulips available are: 'Bleu Aimable' (lilac flushed with purple, and a blue base), 'Snowpeak' (pure white) and 'La Tulipe Noire' (deep purple-black).

    These tulips thrive in good garden soil that is not acid; acid soil needs added lime or chalk to make it more alkaline. Choose a sunny position, with 15cm (6in) of soil over the bulbs, which should be planted in late autumn. Keep them moist during the growing period. When the flowers fade cut off the heads. When the leaves die lift the plant; remove offsets and replant them, storing the parent bulb until late autumn.

Take care
Keep moist while growing. 140♦

Tulip Division 7: Lily-flowered

- Full sun
- Slightly alkaline soil
- Plant 15cm (6in) deep at most

These tulips are noted for their flower shape, being slightly waisted with pointed petals that curl outwards. Blooms open in mid-spring and often reach 20cm (8in) wide. The leaves are green, some with a grey cast; the plants reach 60cm (24in) tall, and look very effective when massed. Colours include white, yellow, orange, red and multicoloured variations. Notable examples are 'Golden Duchess' (deep primrose yellow), 'Mariette' (deep rose, with a glorious texture to the petals), 'Picotee' (white, with a deep rose edging that increases in area as the plant ages) and 'White Triumphator' (a long white bloom).

    These tulips enjoy full sun and a slightly alkaline soil. Plant 15cm (6in) deep in a sunny place in late autumn, and keep it moist while growing. Once the flower petals fall, cut off the heads. When leaves turn yellow, lift the plant, remove the offsets and grow them separately until mature. Use a pesticide and fungicide.

Take care
Add lime to an acid soil. 141♦

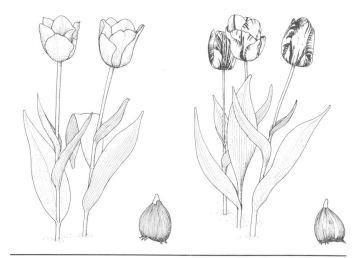

Tulip Division 8: Cottage

- Full sun
- Ordinary slightly alkaline soil
- Plant 15cm (6in) deep at most

This old group of tulips has oval or rounded flowers; petals occasionally have a hint of fringing, and are more loose and open than other forms. The flowers are up to 12.5cm (5in) across, in mid-spring. The plant is up to 90cm (36in) tall, with blue-green leaves. Flower colours include white, yellow, pink, red, lilac and green. Examples to note are 'Dillenburg' (a red-brown tulip that lasts well), 'Mrs John T. Scheepers' (with long oval yellow blooms) and 'Artist' (a strange mixture of green, pink and purple, with the petals partly fringed).

Plant cottage tulips in full sun, in an ordinary soil that is slightly alkaline. Bulbs should be planted in late autumn, 15cm (6in) deep. Keep the soil moist during the growing period. Dead-head the plants to stop seed production and when leaves have turned yellow they can be lifted; remove offsets to a nursery bed, and store parent bulbs for replanting in late autumn. Treat with a pesticide and fungicide to keep plants healthy.

Take care
Keep moist while growing. 141▶

Tulip Division 9: Rembrandt

- Full sun
- Soil that is slightly alkaline
- Plant 15cm (6in) deep at most

These are tulips with 'broken colours', usually Darwin types, which can be seen in old Dutch paintings. The rounded flowers open in mid-spring and are often 12.5cm (5in) wide, with vivid splashes of colour on the petals. The plants stand 75cm (30in) tall, with leaves sometimes having a blue-green cast. Blooms can be white, yellow, orange, red, pink, violet or brown. Two examples are 'May Blossom' (cream and purple) and 'Absalon' (dark coffee-brown and yellow).

Plant bulbs in late autumn, 15cm (6in) deep, in a good garden soil that is slightly alkaline, and in full sun. If the soil is dry at the time of planting, water it well, and leave until the plant starts growing; then keep moist until the leaves turn yellow. Once the flowers have finished, cut off the heads to allow the bulbs to take up food. When the leaves turn yellow, lift the plants, remove and replant the offsets, and store the parent bulbs for replanting in late autumn.

Take care
Dead-head plants after flowering.

 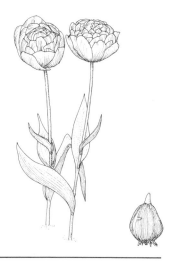

Tulip Division 10: Parrot

- Full sun
- Good limy garden soil
- Plant 15cm (6in) deep at most

Parrot tulips are easily recognized by their heavily fringed and feather-like petals. The blooms are large, reaching 20cm (8in) across, and appear in a range of brilliant white, yellow, pink, orange, red and purple in mid-spring. Plants grow to 60cm (24in) tall. Particularly noteworthy are 'Fantasy' (a soft rose, with pale stripes and featherings of green on the outer petals) and 'Gay Presto' (a brilliant showy bloom of white with scarlet markings).

Place bulbs in a sunny position, 15cm (6in) deep in an ordinary limy soil. Keep moist during the growing period, and when the petals fall off, dead-head the plants. When the leaves turn yellow, plants can be lifted and stored in a dry place until late autumn. Offsets can be removed and replanted in nursery beds to mature. Keep tulips free from attack with a pesticide and fungicide.

Take care
Dead-head to encourage flowering the following year. 142♦

Tulip Division 11: Double Late

- Sunny position
- Limy soil
- Plant 15cm (6in) deep at most

These tulips have huge double flowers that can reach 20cm (8in) wide, in a wide range of colours, and they remain in bloom for a long time. They grow to a height of 60cm (24in), and flowers are white, yellow, orange, pink, red or violets, many multicoloured, with stripes and edgings. Most notable of this group are 'Mount Tacoma' (white), 'Carnaval de Nice' (white with brilliant red stripes) and 'Orange Triumph' (orange with brown shading and yellow fringes, an enormous bloom that often reaches 20cm (8in) across).

Plant bulbs 15cm (6in) deep in a sunny position, although they can stand some shade. Keep the soil moist during the spring growing period, and when the flowers finish cut off the heads to allow the bulbs to take up nourishment for the coming season. When the leaves turn yellow, plants can be lifted, and offsets removed and replanted.

Take care
Watch for damage to blooms from wind or rain. 142-3♦

Tulip Division 12: Kaufmanniana varieties *(Water-lily tulip)*

- Sunny sheltered site
- Well-drained soil
- Plant 15cm (6in) deep at most

These small tulips have been developed from the parent plant *T. kaufmanniana*, which comes from Turkestan. They have fine pointed flowers that open out almost flat, which gives them the appearance of a water-lily. Some open early in spring and they grow to only 10-25cm (4-10in). They are sturdy, and some have attractively striped and mottled leaves. Most have two-coloured flowers almost 10cm (4in) long. These tulips are suitable for rock gardens, the front of borders or containers where they can be left undisturbed. Varieties to note are 'The First' (white with a golden base and red edges), 'Stresa' (red and yellow outside, yellow and brown inside) and 'Shakespeare' (a mixture of pinks and oranges with red shading, only 12.5cm/5 in tall).

Plant in well-drained soil in sunshine, at a depth of 15cm (6in). Keep them moist during spring, and dead-head after flowering.

Take care
Keep moist in spring. 143♦

Tulip Division 13: Fosteriana varieties

- Full sun
- Slightly alkaline soil
- Plant 15cm (6in) deep at most

These are derived from the parent plant *T. fosteriana*, which comes from Central Asia. They grow to a height of 45cm (18in), with large blunt-pointed flowers in reds and yellows in mid-spring, and grey-green leaves. There is only one white variety, 'White Emperor', with large long-lasting blooms. 'Red Emperor' has shiny brilliant red petals with a black base bordered with yellow; and 'Cantata', with orange-red flowers and apple-green leaves, grows only 23cm (9in) tall.

These bulbs thrive on a sunny site in a good garden soil with lime or chalk added. Cover the bulbs with 15cm (6in) of soil in late autumn and keep them moist during the growing season. When the flowers die, cut off their heads to build up the bulb for the following season. Plants may be left in the soil or lifted after the leaves turn yellow; at this time offsets can be removed, and grown on in nursery beds until mature.

Take care
Keep moist while growing. 144♦

Tulip Division 14: Greigii varieties

- Sunny site
- Add lime if soil is acid
- Plant 15cm (6in) deep at most

Tulipa tarda

- Sheltered and sunny position
- Well-drained soil with some lime
- Plant 15cm (6in) deep at most

These hybrids are becoming popular for their decorative leaves and brilliant long-lasting flowers of red, yellow and near-white. The leaves are beautifully marked with stripes and mottles in browny purple, and the short sturdy growth helps plants to stand up to high winds, which makes them ideal for exposed sites. Generally growing to 25cm (10in), they flower in mid-spring. The petals reach 7.5cm (3in) long when the bloom opens fully in direct sunshine.

Where soil is acid, add some lime; where there is heavy clay, add plenty of sharp sand and fibrous material to help drainage. The bulbs should be planted in groups of up to a dozen to give a good display. Pick off the dead heads to build up the bulb for the next year.

Dust soil with an insecticide to deter pests. Most diseases are due to excessive moisture. If disease appears other than rot, destroy bulb.

Take care
Keep the area around the bulbs weed-free.

This small plant from Central Asia is only 10cm (4in) tall and has up to six blooms on each stem; these are star-shaped, and the yellow petals, 5cm (2in) long, have prominent white tips and a green flush on the outside. When planted 7.5cm (3in) apart, they form a carpet of blooms in spring. The narrow leaves are mid-green in colour.

Plant the bulbs in late autumn, in a sunny sheltered position, 15cm (6in) deep in a good well-drained soil that has some lime in it. Plant them in groups of up to a dozen for good effect. During the growing season make sure that the soil does not dry out. After flowering cut off the dead heads to make the plant's strength go into the bulbs. The plants can be left in the soil, but when they become crowded, lift and divide to give them more room. These can also be grown in pots. To keep the plant healthy use a pesticide and fungicide.

Take care
Dead-head the plants to ensure future blooms. 144♦

Tulipa turkestanica

- Sheltered, sunny situation
- Well-drained alkaline soil
- Plant 15cm (6in) deep at most

This plant, a native of Central Asia and North-west China, has a simple six-petalled star-shaped bloom and slender grey-green leaves. The plant grows to a height of 20cm (8in). The flowers are white, with a green and bronze blush on the outside, and up to nine long-lasting blooms over 2.5cm (1in) long are carried by each flower stem in early spring.

Plant bulbs in late autumn in a well-drained soil that has some lime in it, 15cm (6in) deep, in an area where they can receive full sun. During the growing season keep them moist, but when flowers and leaves have faded they prefer to be kept dry. Dead-head the plants to keep the strength going into the bulb rather than for seed production. Plants can be left *in situ* to naturalize, but if they become congested they can be lifted after the leaves turn yellow; remove and replant offsets in a nursery bed, and give parent plants more room. Treat with a pesticide and fungicide.

Take care
Keep moist during spring droughts.

Zantedeschia aethiopica *(Arum lily)*

- Sun or partial shade
- Deep moist soil
- Plant 10cm (4in) deep in soil, 30cm (12in) deep in water

This half-hardy rhizomatous plant will grow out of doors in mild districts, but in less mild areas it should be treated as a pot plant. The leaves are 20cm (8in) long and over 10cm (4in) wide, arrow-shaped and glossy. The 90cm (36in) plant has unusual flowers: an irregular funnel has a central boss (or *spadix*) on which are borne the true flowers (the large cream-coloured funnel is not the actual flower but a *spathe*, or enlarged bud cover).

This is also an aquatic plant that can be grown as deep as 30cm (12in) below water. The deeper the rhizome is planted, the more hardy it seems; in soil, 10cm (4in) gives good protection in winter. Plant in spring in a deep moist soil, in sun or partial shade. To protect the root system during winter, cover plants with a thick layer of straw, bracken or ashes, to keep off the worst of the frosts. In late autumn the plant can be lifted, divided and replanted.

Take care
Guard against frost damage.

Index of Common Names

Credits

Line artwork
The drawings in this book have been prepared by David Papworth.
© Salamander Books Ltd.

Photographs
The majority of the photographs in this book have been taken by Eric Crichton. © Salamander Books Ltd.

Copyright in the following photographs belongs to the suppliers:

Pat Brindley: 14(B), 37, 80, 97, 98(B), 102(T), 104(B)

Eric Crichton: 15(B), 69(B), 78(BR), 98(T), 100-101(B), 106-7(B), 130(TL), 134(T), 140(T), 144(T)

Harry Smith Photographic Collection: 9(R), 34(T), 36(T), 75(T), 99, 104(T), 105(T, B), 131, 137(B)

Editorial assistance
Copy-editing and proof-reading: Maureen Cartwright.

Cyclamen hederifolium

PRINTED IN BELGIUM BY

INTERNATIONAL BOOK PRODUCTION